Catholic Order of the Holy Mass for Kids

A Child-friendly guide to the responses and prayers

Benjamin Blakewell

GRAPEVINE BOOKS

Published by

GRAPEVINE BOOKS

www.grapevinebooks.com

email: contact@grapevinebooks.com

Ordering Information:

Quantity sales: Special discounts are available on quantity purchases by corporations, associations, and others.

For details, reach out to the publisher.

First published by Grapevine Books, 2026

CONTENTS

Chapter 1

What Is the Catholic Mass?

Going to Church: What is Mass and Why Do We Go?

Mass is one of the most important parts of being Catholic. But what exactly is it? Simply put, Mass is a special time when we gather together in church to worship God, pray, and celebrate all that He has done for us. It's kind of like a big family meeting with God as the guest of honor. But it's not just any meeting. It's something that's been happening for thousands of years, and it's super important for us as Catholics.

You've probably already been to Mass before, but did you know that Mass is much more than just sitting in a pew and listening to the priest? It's a time for everyone, kids and adults alike, to come together, hear God's Word, say prayers, sing, and learn more about how much God loves us. And guess what? You're a part of this too! You don't just have to watch from the sidelines, you're in the game!

Mass happens every Sunday, and it's a time we all take a break from the busy world to focus on God. But why do we go to Mass? Well, we go to Mass because it's where we meet Jesus, the Son of God. During Mass, we remember His life and all He did for us, like dying on the cross to save us from sin. When we go to Mass, we thank Jesus for His love, listen to God's Word in the Bible, and share in the special meal called the Eucharist, which means "thanksgiving." It's the way we say "thank you" to God for everything He's given us.

Mass is also a way to spend time with other people who believe in God. The church is like a big family, and when we go to Mass together, we celebrate as one big family. So, the next time you walk into church, know that you're not just sitting there, you're part of something really special. You're part of God's family, and that's pretty cool!

Worship, Sacrifice, and Celebration: A Fun Look at What We Do at Mass

Now, let's dive into why Mass is so important! At Mass, we do three main things: worship, sacrifice, and celebration. They might sound like big words, but don't worry, we're going to break them down so they make sense!

First, let's talk about worship. Worship means showing God how much we love Him. It's like when you do something special for someone you care about, like making a card for your mom or helping your friend with something. When we worship God at Mass, we are telling Him, "We love You, we thank You, and we want to spend time with You." This happens when we pray, sing, and listen to the Bible stories.

In the first part of Mass, we sing songs and say prayers that remind us of how amazing God is. When the priest greets us and says, "The Lord be with you," that's a chance for us to say, "Yes, God, we're here, and we're ready to be with You!" The whole Mass is about spending time with God and showing Him how much we care. You're not just there to listen to the priest, you're there to talk to God and listen to what He has to say to you.

The second big thing we do at Mass is sacrifice. Now, don't worry, a sacrifice doesn't mean giving up something you love. In this case, it's a way of remembering that Jesus gave up His life for us because He loves us so much. When we go to Mass, we remember the sacrifice Jesus made by dying on the cross. Every time we go to Mass, we remember how much He gave up for us. This is why Mass is sometimes called a "sacrifice of praise", we're thanking God for the greatest sacrifice ever made.

But here's something cool: even though Jesus' sacrifice happened a long time ago, at Mass, we get to be part of it in a special way. When the priest says the prayers over the bread and wine, he's remembering what Jesus did at the Last Supper, when He gave His body and blood for us. By offering the bread and wine, we're remembering Jesus' sacrifice, and we're saying, "Thank you, God, for loving us so much."

The last thing we do at Mass is celebrate. Yes, Mass is a big celebration! When we celebrate, we don't just think about the sad parts of Jesus' life, we also remember the happy parts. Like how He rose from the dead and gave us new life. That's what makes Mass such a joyful occasion! We come together to say, "Yay! Thank You, God!" And that's why there are songs, prayers, and even the special meal of the Eucharist (which means "thanksgiving") to celebrate what God has done for us.

In Mass, we celebrate how God is always with us, how He loves us, and how He's given us so many good things. And because God wants us to be happy, Mass is a time for us to feel joy in our hearts. It's like a party for God, and you're invited!

So, now that you know about worship, sacrifice, and celebration, you can see how Mass isn't just a "sit-and-listen" time. It's a time for you to get involved, show God how much you care, remember what Jesus did for us, and celebrate God's love for you. When you come to Mass, you're taking part in something really special, a chance to be close to God and celebrate His amazing love!

Meeting Jesus at Mass: How He is Really There with Us

Have you ever been to a party where everyone is excited to see the guest of honor? At Mass, Jesus is like the special guest, and He's there with us, but in a way that's even more amazing than we can see with our eyes.

You might be thinking, "How is Jesus really there at Mass? I don't see Him!" Well, that's because Jesus is present in a special way that's different from how we see other people. At Mass, Jesus is truly with us, even though we can't physically see Him. He's not standing in front of us like a person, but He's still there in a very real way!

Here's how that happens: During the Mass, especially when we celebrate the Eucharist (which is the part where we receive the bread and wine), something amazing takes place. The bread and wine become the body and blood of Jesus. This might sound a little confusing, but it's really important! The bread and wine don't just stay the same. They actually change into Jesus Himself. This is called the Real Presence of Jesus. It's like Jesus is coming to meet us in a way that we can receive Him into our hearts.

You can think of it like this: Imagine you have a favorite toy, and when you look at it, you see it as it is. But if someone were to take that toy and turn it into something else, like a shiny new superhero figure, you would know that it's still the same toy, but it's been changed into something new. In the same way, the bread and wine at Mass are changed into Jesus, even though they still look like bread and wine.

Why does this happen? Jesus wants to be close to us. He loves us so much that He gives Himself to us in the Eucharist, so we can be close to Him, just like a friend who wants to be near you. When we receive Communion, it's not just a snack. It's a special moment where we are really connecting with Jesus. He comes into our hearts, and we get to be with Him in a special way. This helps us grow in our friendship with Him.

It's kind of like when you call or video chat with a friend who's far away. You can't hug them, but you can still talk and share time together. At Mass, even though we can't see Jesus physically, we get to be with Him through the Eucharist. And when we say "Amen" before receiving Communion, we are saying, "Yes, I believe that Jesus is really with me!"

But how do we know Jesus is really there if we can't see Him? Well, it's all about faith. Faith means believing in something even if we can't see it with our eyes. Just like we believe in the air we breathe even though we can't see it, we believe that Jesus is with us in the Eucharist. We don't need to see Him to know He's there. Our faith helps us trust that He is.

When you receive Communion, it's also a reminder that Jesus is always with you, not just at Mass, but all the time! When you face tough days, or when you feel lonely, you can remember that Jesus is with you in your heart, and He wants to help you. By coming to Mass and meeting Jesus there, you are filling up your heart with His love, just like how you might feel full after eating your favorite food.

So next time you're at Mass and you hear the priest say, "This is My Body," remember that it's not just a symbol but Jesus Himself, really present with us, in a way that we can receive into our hearts. Mass is the best place to meet Jesus, and He's waiting for you, ready to give you His love, peace, and strength. *It's like getting a big hug from Jesus every time you go!*

Chapter 2

The Story of Mass

Imagine you're sitting at a big table with your closest friends, eating a meal and laughing together. You feel happy and safe, surrounded by love. Now, imagine that this meal is so special that it's remembered for centuries. Well, that's exactly what happened at the Last Supper, a meal that Jesus shared with His disciples before He died.

A Long Time Ago: The Last Supper and How Mass Started

The Last Supper wasn't just any regular dinner. It was the first Mass! Jesus knew that He was about to do something incredibly important for all of us, so He decided to make this meal extra special. He took some bread and wine, and instead of just eating it like a regular meal, He did something amazing: He blessed the bread and wine and said, "This is My Body" and "This is My Blood." Can you imagine being there? It was like He was sharing Himself with them in a way that was beyond words! Jesus gave Himself to His friends in that moment, and that's exactly what happens at Mass today. Jesus gives Himself to us in a special way.

After this special meal, Jesus told His disciples to do this in remembrance of Me. He was telling them to continue sharing this special meal, just like He did with them. That's how the very first Mass began! Jesus wanted His disciples and everyone who would follow Him to keep coming together to remember Him, celebrate Him, and share His love with the world.

The idea of having Mass didn't start with just a big meal. Jesus wanted us to celebrate and remember Him every time we gather. This is why we have Mass today, because Jesus asked us to keep doing this. So, every time we go to Mass, it's like we're going back in time to that very first meal with Jesus. It's a way to connect with Him, to hear His words, and to remember His great love for us.

Mass became more than just a meal, though. Over time, the early Christians started gathering together for worship and prayer, just like Jesus showed them. They shared the Eucharist (the bread and wine), listened to God's Word, and gave thanks to God. And as people started sharing the message of Jesus around the world, they continued to celebrate Mass wherever they went.

Now, every Sunday (or sometimes more often), we come together to celebrate Mass, just like Jesus told us to. Mass is a special meeting where we can talk to God, hear from Him, and be close to Him. The best part? We are doing what Jesus asked us to do when He said, "Do this in remembrance of Me." It's like we're getting to hang out with Jesus every time we celebrate Mass!

Old and New Mass: Latin and Modern Mass

Okay, so now you know how Mass began, but have you ever wondered why some people at church still speak a language that sounds like it's from another time, like Latin? Well, let's travel back in time to learn about the old and new ways of celebrating Mass!

The Old Mass: Latin Mass

Many, many years ago, almost everyone in the world spoke Latin, a language that was used by the Church. For centuries, the Latin Mass was the way people celebrated Mass all over the world. Even if you didn't speak Latin, you would still be at Mass, and you'd hear the priest speaking in Latin, singing prayers in Latin, and even responding to God in Latin. It might sound a little strange to think about now, but back then, it was the language that brought everyone together, no matter where they lived.

Latin is kind of like a secret code that the Church used to make sure that everyone, everywhere, could understand the same things about God. If you went to a church in Italy, or one in the United States, or even one in Mexico, you would hear the same Latin words! It was a way to make sure everyone was part of the same global Church. You'd also notice a lot of beautiful singing during the Latin Mass, especially during special parts of the Mass like the Gloria and Holy, Holy, Holy. Even though you might not have understood the words exactly, the music and the rhythm helped you feel close to God.

But as time went on, the world began to change. People started speaking different languages in different countries, and not everyone could understand Latin anymore. Even though Latin was still really important, the Church realized that it was important for people to be able to understand what was happening in the Mass and to feel more involved. This led to the changes that came with the New Mass.

The New Mass: Modern Mass

In the 1960s, there was a big change in how the Church celebrated Mass.

The Church decided to make the Mass more understandable for everyone, so they started celebrating Mass in the language that people spoke in their own countries. For example, if you lived in an English-speaking country like the United States, you would hear Mass in English instead of Latin. In other countries, they started using Spanish, French, and other languages.

This change made Mass feel more personal. You could understand what the priest was saying and be more involved in the prayers. Imagine hearing the priest say, "The Lord be with you," and you can understand it and respond, "And with your spirit!" That might feel much more like a conversation with God, right?

The New Mass also allowed for more involvement from everyone in the church. Now, people could sing songs in their own language, say prayers together, and really understand what was happening. This made Mass more of a community experience because everyone could actively participate, whether it was by singing, saying the prayers, or even reading the Bible passages.

But even though the New Mass is celebrated in different languages, it still has a lot of the same important parts that the Latin Mass had. For example, we still have the Introductory Rites, the Liturgy of the Word, the Eucharist (the special meal), and the Concluding Rites, just like in the Old Mass. The language has changed, but the main parts of Mass are still the same. So, in a way, the New Mass is like a modern version of the Old Mass, and both are important because they help us meet Jesus and worship God together as a family.

Why Both Matter

Both the Old Mass (Latin Mass) and the New Mass (Modern Mass) are special ways of celebrating Mass. The Latin Mass is beautiful and timeless, and it helps remind us of the long history of the Church. It brings people from all over the world together through the same ancient language. The New Mass allows us to be more connected with the prayers and songs, because we understand them in our own language. Both ways of celebrating Mass help us grow in faith and love for Jesus.

No matter what language we speak or what style of Mass we attend, the important thing is that we're gathering to worship God and meet Jesus. And that's what makes Mass so special! Whether it's in Latin or English, it's all about being with Jesus, listening to His Word, and celebrating His love. And the best part? No matter which way the Mass is celebrated, Jesus is always there with us, ready to pour His love into our hearts.

So, now you know a little more about where Mass started and how it's changed over time! Whether it's the old Latin Mass or the modern Mass we celebrate today, we're all part of the same beautiful tradition that Jesus began with His first disciples. Every time you go to Mass, you're taking part in something that connects you to Christians all around the world and throughout history. *How cool is that?*

Chapter 3

The Four Main Parts of Mass

Mass is more than just a gathering at church; it's an experience, an adventure, and a chance to meet God. When we go to Mass, we follow a special order of events. The Mass is divided into four main parts: the Introductory Rites, the Liturgy of the Word, the Liturgy of the Eucharist, and the Concluding Rites. Each part is important because it helps us connect with God in a different way. Let's explore the first two parts: what we do at the beginning and how we hear God's Word.

What We Do at the Beginning: The Introductory Rites

When you walk into church and sit down, you might notice that everyone is talking quietly, finding their seats, or maybe even saying hi to someone they know. The beginning of Mass is a time to get ready for something really special! This part is called the Introductory Rites, and it helps us get into the right mindset for the rest of Mass. It's like when you get ready for a big game or an exciting event. Mass deserves a little preparation!

First, the priest comes up to the altar and greets everyone. The priest says, "The Lord be with you," and we respond with, "And with your spirit." This simple greeting is super important because it's a reminder that God is with us. When the priest says, "The Lord be with you," it's like he's welcoming you to the party, God's party!

After that, we have a song or hymn. This is when everyone sings together to lift up our hearts. Singing at the beginning of Mass is special because it helps us get in the mood to worship. Imagine you're about to see your best friend, and you sing a fun song just to get excited! That's what this song does at Mass. It helps us get ready to meet Jesus, and we sing because we love Him. Whether it's a joyful song or one that's quiet and peaceful, it helps set the tone for what's about to happen.

The next part of the Introductory Rites is the Penitential Act. This might sound fancy, but it's really simple! The Penitential Act is when we ask God to forgive us for any mistakes we've made. Everyone, even the priest, says a prayer called the Confiteor: "I confess to almighty God and to you, my brothers and sisters, that I have greatly sinned." This prayer is like saying, "Sorry, God!" It's a way to start fresh. It's important to say sorry to God so we can focus on the rest of Mass without any distractions.

When we say this prayer, we remember that Jesus loves us, forgives us, and helps us do better.

After the Penitential Act, we all sing or say the Gloria, which is another beautiful prayer to praise God. The Gloria says, "Glory to God in the highest, and on earth peace to people of good will." It's like shouting "Hooray!" for God, and we say it together as a big group. This prayer reminds us that God is the King of the world and that we want to share His peace with everyone.

Then, the priest prays a special prayer called the Collect, which gathers all of our prayers together. This is where the priest asks God to hear the prayers of everyone in the church. It's like making a wish together as a group, asking God for His help and guidance during the Mass. After this, we're ready to move on to the next part of the Mass—the Liturgy of the Word!

Reading and Listening to God's Word: The Liturgy of the Word

Now that we're ready, it's time to hear from God! The Liturgy of the Word is the part of Mass when we listen to the Bible. It's called the Liturgy of the Word because we're getting to hear God's Word. Imagine that the Bible is like God's letter to us, and we're reading it together as a family. This part of Mass is like sitting down with a friend and listening to their advice. God speaks to us through the Bible, and we need to listen carefully to what He has to say.

First, there's the First Reading, which usually comes from the Old Testament, the first part of the Bible. It's like hearing a story about someone from the past who followed God. Sometimes, the first reading is about someone who did something amazing for God, like Noah or Moses, and other times it's about challenges people faced and how they trusted in God. After the reading, there's a Psalm, which is a song from the Bible. The Psalm is usually a prayer that praises God. We either listen to the choir sing it, or we sing along together as a congregation. It's a way of responding to God's Word with love and joy.

Then comes the Second Reading, which is usually from the New Testament, the part of the Bible that talks about Jesus and the early Christian Church. This reading might talk about how to live a good life or how to love others the way Jesus loves us. After this reading, we stand up for the Gospel. The Gospel is the most important part of the Liturgy of the Word, because it tells the story of Jesus.

The Gospel is usually read by the priest or deacon, and it's always about something Jesus did or taught. When the Gospel is read, everyone stands up to show respect for the words of Jesus. It's like standing for a king or queen! Before the Gospel reading, we sing the Gospel Acclamation, a short song that gets us ready to hear the good news about Jesus. The priest or deacon then says, "The Lord be with you," and everyone responds, "And with your spirit." Then he says, "A reading from the Gospel according to [name of the Evangelist]," and we all make a sign of the cross on our foreheads, lips, and hearts. This is a way to say, "Jesus, please help me understand and remember Your words!"

After the Gospel is read, the priest gives a homily. This is when the priest talks about the readings and explains them to us. He helps us understand how we can live better lives by following what God has taught us. It's kind of like a mini-lesson or a fun story that shows us how to love God and each other. The homily is the part of Mass where the priest helps us see how the Bible connects to our lives today.

After the homily, everyone professes their faith by saying the Nicene Creed or Apostles' Creed. This is when we remind ourselves what we believe in. The Creed is a statement of faith that says, "Yes, I believe in God, I believe in Jesus, and I believe in the Holy Spirit." Saying the Creed is like making a promise to God that we believe in Him and want to follow Him. It's a way of saying, "I'm part of God's family, and I trust Him!"

Once we say the Creed, it's time to pray for others. This is when we pray for people who are sick, for our families, for our friends, and for everyone around the world. The priest says a prayer, and everyone responds with "Lord, hear our prayer." It's our chance to ask God to help everyone we care about, and even those we don't know, because we want to bring God's love to everyone.

Now that we've heard God's Word and prayed together, we're ready to move on to the next part of Mass, the Liturgy of the Eucharist, where we meet Jesus in the special meal. But before we get there, remember how important the Liturgy of the Word is! It helps us hear from God, understand His love, and get ready for the rest of Mass. Every time we hear the Bible, we get to connect with God in a new and exciting way. How cool is that?

Now that we've listened to God's Word, it's time for the most special part of Mass: the Liturgy of the Eucharist! This is where we say "thank you" to God in the most amazing way possible. Remember how at the beginning of Mass, we heard about the Last Supper, where Jesus shared the bread and wine with His disciples? Well, the Liturgy of the Eucharist is where we do the same thing! It's the moment when we are closest to Jesus during Mass.

Let's start by talking about what happens during the Eucharist. The priest brings the bread and wine to the altar, just like the disciples did at the Last Supper. But here's the really cool part. Through the priest's prayer, the bread and wine are transformed into the body and blood of Jesus. Now, it's not like the bread suddenly turns into a piece of Jesus you can touch with your hands or the wine turns into a visible cup of blood. Instead, it's a mystery! The bread and wine still look the same, but they are now truly Jesus. This is called the Real Presence of Jesus in the Eucharist, and it's a big deal! You're receiving Jesus in the most special way, and that's something that happens every time you go to Mass.

After the priest has set the bread and wine on the altar, he says a prayer called the Eucharistic Prayer. This prayer is really important because it asks God to bless the bread and wine, and to turn them into Jesus' body and blood. The priest then holds up the bread and says, "This is My Body," and everyone responds, "Amen!" This "Amen" means, "Yes, I believe that this is really Jesus, and I accept Him into my heart."

Then, the priest does the same thing with the wine. He says, "This is the chalice of My Blood," and once again, we respond, "Amen!" It's like we're saying, "Yes, Jesus, we believe in You, and we thank You for giving Yourself to us."

But it doesn't stop there! After the Eucharistic Prayer, we all join together to say the Our Father, a prayer that Jesus taught His disciples. This is a prayer where we ask God to help us with everything in life and to give us strength. When we say the Our Father, it's like we're all coming together as one big family, asking God to take care of us and the whole world.

Next comes the Sign of Peace. This is such a beautiful moment because we're all sharing God's peace with each other. The priest says, "Peace be with you," and we respond, "And with your spirit." Then, everyone turns to each other, shakes hands, or gives a wave or smile. It's a reminder that we're not just there to pray by ourselves, but we're part of a bigger family, the Church, and we should share God's love and peace with everyone around us.

Once we've shared the peace, it's time for Holy Communion! This is the part when we get to receive the body and blood of Jesus in the form of the bread and wine. The priest or Eucharistic minister holds up the host (the body of Christ) and says, "The Body of Christ," and we say, "Amen." This is a way to say, "Yes, I believe Jesus is really present, and I welcome Him into my heart." When we receive the Eucharist, it's like we're being connected to Jesus in the deepest, most amazing way.

For some of you, this might be your first time receiving Communion, and that's a very exciting moment! But even if you've already received Communion many times, remember that every time is a special moment where you're receiving God's love into your heart. It's a way for us to be closer to Jesus and feel His love for us. Think of it like receiving a hug from God, who's always there to help and guide you.

When everyone has received Communion, the priest may say a prayer, and we all give thanks to God for this special gift. At the end of this part, we return to our seats, and we spend a moment in quiet prayer, thanking Jesus for coming into our hearts and being with us in such a special way. This is the time when you can tell Jesus what's on your heart and listen to what He wants to say to you.

Saying Goodbye: The Concluding Rites

After the incredible experience of receiving the Eucharist, Mass is almost over, but there's still one last part: the Concluding Rites! This is when we say goodbye to each other and go out into the world, ready to spread the love and peace we received at Mass.

The first thing that happens during the Concluding Rites is a short prayer, where the priest thanks God for the blessings we received during Mass. It's like when you have a fun party with friends, and at the end, you say, "Thank you for coming, and I hope you had a good time!" This prayer is a way of thanking God for everything He's given us and asking Him to help us use the strength we received to do good things.

After the prayer, the priest gives us a final blessing. This is an important moment because the priest is asking God to bless us and keep us safe until we come back to Mass again. The priest says, "The Lord be with you," and we respond, "And with your spirit." Then, the priest gives us a blessing, saying, "May Almighty God bless you, the Father, and the Son, and the Holy Spirit." This blessing is like God's big hug for everyone in the church, reminding us that He is with us always, helping us through the week.

Then, the priest says, "Go in peace, glorifying the Lord by your life." This is the part where Mass ends, but it's also the part where we get a big job to do! The priest is telling us to go out into the world and share the love and peace we've received at Mass. It's like when you finish reading a really good book, and now you get to go out and tell everyone about it. The love of God is something that's meant to be shared, and the priest is reminding us to live in a way that shows others how much we love Jesus.

As we walk out of church, we might talk to our family or friends, or we might just think about what we've learned during Mass. It's a time to reflect on the peace and joy we received and how we can be better people because of it. Mass might be over, but it's like taking the love of God with us, wherever we go!

And that's how Mass ends: with a prayer, a blessing, and a sending forth to bring God's love to everyone around us. It's like the end of a good story, but it's also the beginning of a new adventure, living out the love and peace we've received at Mass!

Mass is an amazing experience because we get to meet Jesus, listen to God's Word, say thank you to God, and receive His love in the Eucharist. After all of that, we go out into the world, ready to live like Jesus and share His love with others. Every part of Mass is important, and each one helps us grow closer to God and live our faith in the world around us. How awesome is that? So, next time you go to Mass, remember: it's not just about being there; it's about what you take with you when you leave. God's love in your heart, ready to be shared!

Chapter 4

Introductory Rites

When you walk into church for Mass, you might notice a lot of people chatting, getting comfortable, or sitting quietly. Everyone is getting ready for something amazing—Mass! But before we jump into the most important parts, we start with the Introductory Rites. This is the part where we get ourselves ready to meet God, and it sets the tone for everything that happens next. It's like when you get ready for a big game, a fun party, or an exciting event. You need a little warm-up to get into the right mindset. So, let's explore what happens during the Introductory Rites at Mass, and how they help us focus on God and prepare our hearts for the celebration ahead.

Singing and Saying "Hello": Entrance Procession and Greeting

The Entrance Procession is the first thing that happens when Mass begins. This is when the priest and other ministers (like deacons or altar servers) walk to the altar. They usually carry something important, like the Book of the Gospels, or they might be holding candles. This procession is a way of saying, "We're starting something special!" It's like when the lights go down at a concert, and the band walks on stage. Everyone gets excited because something important is about to happen.

But don't worry, you're not just sitting there watching! You get to be a part of it, too! As the procession happens, we all stand and sing a song. This is the Entrance Hymn, and it's our way of saying, "We're ready to begin!" The song might be joyful and loud, or it could be more peaceful and quiet, depending on the mood. But whatever the song is, it helps us focus our hearts and minds on God. Singing together is like the first big step into Mass, and it helps us connect as a community.

The song also prepares us to greet God. When we sing or say prayers at the beginning, we're not just going through the motions; we're actively opening our hearts to God. You know how when you see a friend after a long day or a busy week, you greet them with a "Hello!"? That's what we do during the Entrance Procession and Greeting. We're greeting God and saying, "Here I am, ready to meet You!"

As the priest reaches the altar, he says, "In the name of the Father, and of the Son, and of the Holy Spirit," and we respond, "Amen." That's our way of saying, "I agree, I believe in God, and I'm ready to be here with You." After that, the priest might give a short greeting, like, "The Lord be with you," and we all respond, "And with your spirit." It's kind of like saying, "Hi! I'm happy to be here with you, God!" This greeting is a reminder that God is with us as we begin our time of worship together. It helps us remember that Mass isn't just about us; it's about being with God, talking to Him, and listening to what He has to say.

Saying Sorry: Penitential Act (Fun Rhymes and Easy Prayers)

After we say "hello" to God and get ready for Mass, the next thing we do is called the Penitential Act. You might be wondering, "What does 'penitential' mean?" Well, it's just a fancy word for saying "sorry." When we do the Penitential Act, we take a moment to say sorry for the things we've done wrong. Even though we don't want to mess up, we all make mistakes from time to time. Maybe we didn't listen, maybe we weren't as kind as we should've been, or maybe we hurt someone's feelings without meaning to. Whatever it is, the Penitential Act is a chance for us to ask God to forgive us, so we can start fresh.

You might think that saying "sorry" at Mass sounds kind of serious, and it can be. But don't worry, it doesn't have to be scary! Saying sorry to God doesn't mean we're in trouble; it's a way to make things right and remind ourselves that God loves us no matter what. Think of it like when you accidentally bump into someone and say, "Oops, sorry!" It's a quick moment to say, "I didn't mean to do that, but I want to do better next time." The Penitential Act is kind of like that. It's a chance to clear our hearts and get ready for the rest of Mass with a clean slate.

The priest will start by saying, "Brothers and sisters, let us acknowledge our sins, and so prepare ourselves to celebrate the sacred mysteries." This is like saying, "Let's take a moment to think about the things we've done that weren't right, so we can be ready to meet God." Then, we all say a prayer called the Confiteor, which means, "I confess." It starts like this: "I confess to almighty God and to you, my brothers and sisters, that I have greatly sinned..." As we say this prayer, we're talking to God, telling Him, "I know I've made mistakes, but I'm sorry, and I want to be better."

After we say the Confiteor, we all take a moment to quietly think about the things we might need to say sorry for. Maybe you remember something you did wrong, or maybe you're just thinking about the times you didn't live up to the person God wants you to be. This is your chance to reflect on those things in your heart and ask for forgiveness.

Then comes the fun part! We say a prayer called the Kyrie Eleison (which means "Lord, have mercy"). It's like a little chant where we say, "Lord, have mercy. Christ, have mercy. Lord, have mercy." This is our way of asking God to forgive us, and it's kind of like singing a song of forgiveness. It's a reminder that God is always ready to forgive us, and He loves us no matter what.

Once we've said sorry to God, we know that He forgives us and is ready to help us be better. We don't have to worry about being punished. Instead, we can feel peaceful and ready for what's next in Mass because we're starting with a clean heart. After the Penitential Act, we're ready to move on to the rest of the Mass, where we'll pray, listen, and be close to God again.

Why the Introductory Rites Matter

You might be wondering, "Why do we have all these steps at the beginning of Mass? Can't we just get to the good stuff?" Well, the Introductory Rites might seem like they're just a warm-up, but they're actually really important because they help us get in the right frame of mind. They help us prepare our hearts for everything we're about to experience during Mass.

The Entrance Procession and Greeting remind us that we're coming together as a community, united by our love for God. We're not just at Mass by ourselves; we're part of a big family, the Church! The Penitential Act helps us say sorry and get rid of anything that might be holding us back from being close to God. It's like cleaning up your room before you play, so you can have fun without distractions. And, of course, the songs and prayers are there to remind us that this is a special time where we get to connect with God and with each other.

So, next time you're at Mass and you're standing during the Entrance Procession, or saying the Penitential Act, remember: these are the steps that help us open our hearts and minds to God. They help us start Mass in the best way possible, ready to meet Jesus, hear His Word, and experience His love.

Prayers We Say Together: Gloria and Collect

After the Entrance Procession, the greeting, and the penitential act, we're ready to get into the heart of Mass! There are a couple of prayers we say together during the Introductory Rites: the Gloria and the Collect. These prayers help us focus on God and prepare us for the rest of the Mass. Let's take a look at these prayers and why they're so special.

The Gloria: Praising God Together

The Gloria is a joyful prayer of praise and thanksgiving to God. It's a prayer that reminds us just how amazing God is and how much He deserves our worship. Think of it like a cheer you'd do at a game, but instead of cheering for a team, we're cheering for God! When we say the Gloria, we are telling God how much we love Him and how grateful we are for everything He's done for us.

The Gloria begins with the words, "Glory to God in the highest, and on earth peace to people of good will." These words come from the angels who appeared to the shepherds when Jesus was born, announcing the good news. So, when we say the Gloria, we are joining the angels in singing praises to God for His love and goodness.

As we go through the prayer, we say things like, "We praise You, we bless You, we adore You, we glorify You, we give You thanks for Your great glory." These words are like a big thank you to God for all He has done. It's important to remember that God is not just our Creator, He's also our Father, and He loves us deeply. Saying the Gloria reminds us of this love and helps us connect with God's greatness.

In Mass, the Gloria is a way to start our time of worship by focusing on God. It's not just a song or a prayer we say by habit. It's a chance to pause and really think about how awesome God is and how much we appreciate Him. Whether we're singing it loud or quietly praying it in our hearts, the Gloria helps set the tone for the whole Mass. It gets us excited and ready to hear God's Word and share in the Eucharist.

The Collect: Gathering Our Prayers

After the Gloria, the priest prays a special prayer called the Collect. This is a prayer where the priest gathers all of our thoughts and prayers together. Have you ever gone to a big meeting or event where someone asks everyone to take a moment and share their thoughts? The Collect is like that! The priest asks God to listen to the prayers of everyone in the church and to help us with whatever we need. The priest may say something like, "Let us pray" before he starts the prayer, and then we all quietly listen while he prays for all of us.

The Collect helps us remember that we are not alone in our prayers. Even though we might have different things we want to pray about, we are all united in our worship of God. The priest is like a bridge, connecting us to God as he prays for us all. When the priest finishes the Collect, he says, "Through our Lord Jesus Christ, Your Son, who lives and reigns with You in the unity of the Holy Spirit, one God, forever and ever." We respond, "Amen," which means, "Yes, we agree!" Saying "Amen" shows that we agree with everything the priest just prayed for, and that we believe God will answer our prayers.

So, whether we're saying the Gloria, which is all about praising God, or we're listening to the Collect, which gathers all our prayers together, these prayers help us get our hearts and minds ready for the rest of Mass. They are moments to focus on God's greatness and to ask for His help. As we go through the rest of Mass, it's important to remember that these prayers aren't just words. They're ways for us to connect with God and invite Him into our lives.

What Do We Do With Our Bodies? Gestures and Movements at Mass

Now that we've talked about the prayers we say together, let's look at what we do with our bodies during Mass. Have you ever noticed that when people are at Mass, they're not just sitting still the whole time? We stand, sit, kneel, bow, and even make the sign of the cross. Each of these movements has a special meaning and helps us focus on God in different ways. Let's explore why these gestures and movements are so important during Mass.

Standing: Showing Respect and Readiness

One of the most common things we do at Mass is standing. You'll notice that we stand for parts of the Mass like the Gospel, the prayers, and sometimes the Eucharistic Prayer. But why do we stand? Standing at Mass is a way of showing respect for God and His Word. Imagine standing up when a teacher or a leader enters a room. It's a way to honor them. When we stand at Mass, we're honoring God, who is the King of the universe! It's also a sign of readiness. We stand to show that we are ready to listen to God's Word, ready to receive His love, and ready to worship Him.

Sitting: Listening and Reflecting

When we sit, it's usually during the readings from the Bible or during the homily (the priest's talk). Sitting is a sign that we're taking time to listen and reflect. It's like when you sit down to listen to a story, or when you're really paying attention to something important. When we sit at Mass, it helps us focus on what's being said and gives us time to think about how God's Word can be part of our lives. It's a chance to open our hearts and minds to what God wants to teach us, without distractions.

Kneeling: Showing Reverence and Prayer

You might have noticed that we kneel at certain parts of Mass, especially during the Eucharistic Prayer and when we're about to receive Communion. Kneeling is a sign of respect, reverence, and prayer. In many cultures, when you kneel, it's a way of showing deep respect or honor for someone important. When we kneel during Mass, we're showing God how much we love and respect Him. It's also a way to humble ourselves and acknowledge that God is the greatest.

Kneeling helps us focus on God and remember that He is the center of everything. It's a moment to pause, reflect, and prepare ourselves to receive His love in the Eucharist. When you kneel, it's like saying, "God, I am here to worship You, and I am ready to receive Your gift."

Bow: Showing Respect to God's Presence

Another gesture we make at Mass is the bow. You'll see people bowing during certain parts of the Mass, especially when they pass the altar or when the priest mentions the name of Jesus. Bows are a way of showing respect. It's a little like saying, "Thank You" to God for all He's done for us. We don't bow because we're forced to, we bow because we want to honor God and show our gratitude.

Bowing also reminds us of how important the altar is. The altar is where we meet Jesus in the Eucharist, and it's a place where we remember the sacrifice He made for us. By bowing, we're showing that we respect the altar and what it represents, Jesus' love and sacrifice for us.

Sign of the Cross: Inviting God Into Our Lives

One of the first gestures we make at Mass is the Sign of the Cross. You probably do this every time you pray, but do you know what it means? When we make the Sign of the Cross, we are reminding ourselves that we are part of God's family, the Father, the Son, and the Holy Spirit. It's like saying, "God, I belong to You, and I want You to be with me always." The Sign of the Cross is a powerful symbol that reminds us of Jesus' sacrifice on the cross, His love for us, and how He is always with us.

Each time we make the Sign of the Cross, we are starting our prayer or our time at Mass with God. It's a way of welcoming God into our hearts and reminding ourselves that we are never alone.

Why Gestures Matter

You might wonder why all of these gestures are so important. After all, we could just sit and listen to the Mass without moving, right? But the reason we use gestures and movements is because they help us express what's in our hearts. They help us show respect, love, and reverence for God. When we stand, sit, kneel, bow, or make the Sign of the Cross, we're not just doing actions for the sake of doing them. We're showing God that we are engaged in worship, that we want to be close to Him, and that we're ready to learn and grow in faith.

These movements also help us pay attention and focus. Just like when you stand up to listen to something important, or when you sit down to think carefully, the movements at Mass help us connect with God in a deeper way. They make the Mass come alive and help us experience everything more fully.

Next time you go to Mass, pay attention to the gestures you make, and think about what each one means. Whether you're standing, sitting, kneeling, or making the Sign of the Cross, each movement helps you focus on God and show your love and respect for Him. The gestures we make during Mass help us enter into the experience of worship and connect with God in a meaningful way. And the best part? You get to do all of this with your community, as part of God's family!

Chapter 5
Liturgy of the Word

Mass is filled with amazing moments, and one of the most important parts is the Liturgy of the Word. This is the time during Mass when we listen to God's Word, hear stories from the Bible, and respond to what God is saying to us. It's a time to pay close attention because God is speaking directly to us, guiding us with His wisdom and love. Let's dive into two key parts of the Liturgy of the Word: the First Reading and Singing Psalms. These are some of the most powerful moments of Mass, and they help us connect with God in a deeper way.

First Reading: Listening to Stories from the Bible

The First Reading is the very first passage we hear during the Liturgy of the Word. It comes from the Old Testament, which is the first part of the Bible. This part of the Bible tells us about the history of God's people, from the very beginning of creation to the time before Jesus was born. It's like hearing a story about how everything began and how God has always been with His people, guiding them through life.

When the reader or priest says the First Reading, it's like opening up a window into the past. We get to hear stories about people like Noah, Abraham, Moses, and the prophets. These people were chosen by God to help guide His people and show them how to live according to God's will. The First Reading can sometimes be a little bit like an adventure story, filled with challenges, victories, and important lessons.

For example, you might hear about Noah building the ark and saving the animals from the flood, or how Moses led the Israelites out of Egypt. These stories are not just cool history lessons, though. They are meant to teach us important lessons about trust, faith, and God's love. Even though the stories happened a long time ago, they still matter today because they show us how God worked in the lives of His people, and how He still works in our lives today.

One thing to keep in mind during the First Reading is that these stories are God's messages to us. Just like we listen to a teacher or parent when they share advice, the Bible stories are God's way of teaching us how to live a good life. Even though the stories are ancient, the lessons they teach are timeless. Listening to the First Reading is like tuning into a conversation with God. He's saying, "Here's how you can live with love and kindness," and we can listen and learn from these amazing stories.

After the First Reading, the reader will say, "The Word of the Lord," and everyone responds, "Thanks be to God." This is our way of saying, "Thank you, God, for sharing this story with us. We're ready to learn from it." It's a little like saying "thank you" after a great lesson or story. We want to show God that we appreciate His Word and are ready to take it to heart.

Singing Psalms: What Are Psalms and Why Do We Sing Them?

After the First Reading, it's time for the Psalm, which is a special part of Mass where we all sing together. The Psalms are songs and prayers that come from the Book of Psalms in the Bible. They were written by King David and other people who wanted to express their love for God, ask for His help, and praise Him for His greatness. The Psalms are like the "songbook" of the Bible!

What's really cool about the Psalms is that they speak to us in a very personal way. Some of the Psalms are about joy and praise, where the writer thanks God for everything He's done. Other Psalms are more serious or even sad, where the writer is asking God for help or crying out to Him during tough times. Because the Psalms are filled with emotions, they can connect with us in many different ways. If you're feeling happy, you can sing a joyful Psalm to praise God. If you're feeling sad or worried, there are Psalms that help you express your feelings and ask God for His help.

During Mass, the Responsorial Psalm is often sung right after the First Reading. The priest or cantor will lead the Psalm, and the congregation (that's everyone in the church!) will respond with a refrain, like "The Lord is my shepherd, there is nothing I shall want" or "Praise the Lord, all you nations." It's a way for everyone to join together and respond to the Word of God in song. Singing the Psalm helps us remember the message from the First Reading and reflect on it in our hearts.

You might be wondering, "Why do we sing the Psalms instead of just reading them?" Well, singing adds something special to the experience. When we sing, we're not just saying the words; we're lifting them up to God with our voices. It's like a big, happy thank you to God for His love and all the good things He has done for us. Singing the Psalms also helps us feel more connected to each other. When we all sing together, we're united in our love for God, and it creates a sense of community. Plus, singing is just plain fun!

The Psalms also have a way of helping us express our feelings, even if we don't know exactly how to pray. If you're feeling scared, anxious, or unsure, there's a Psalm that can give you the words to speak to God. If you're feeling really happy, the Psalms can help you sing your praise. It's like having a conversation with God in music, where you can share anything that's on your heart. And even if you're not sure how to sing, you can still **listen** and let the music fill you with peace and joy.

Why the Liturgy of the Word Matters

The Liturgy of the Word is such an important part of Mass because it's when God speaks to us directly. Just like you would listen carefully to a teacher or a friend who has something important to say, we listen carefully during the readings and the Psalms because God is sharing His wisdom with us. The First Reading, the Psalm, and the Gospel are all ways that God helps us learn how to live, love, and trust Him. By listening to these stories and prayers, we're opening our hearts to God's message.

The Liturgy of the Word also reminds us that God is always with us, guiding us. Even though the stories in the Bible happened a long time ago, they still speak to us today because they show us what it means to live with faith, love, and hope. Whether we're hearing about Moses leading the people of Israel, or David writing songs of praise to God, the message is clear: God loves us, He's always there for us, and He wants to help us live our best lives.

Another reason the Liturgy of the Word is so powerful is because it's something we do together. When we listen to the readings, sing the Psalms, and say the prayers, we're joining in a worldwide conversation with God. Christians all around the world are listening to the same Scriptures, singing the same songs, and responding to God's love together. It's like being part of a huge family of believers who all share the same goal: to grow closer to God and learn from His Word.

So, next time you're at Mass and the First Reading begins, listen carefully to the story. It's not just any story, it's God's story, meant to help you understand more about Him and His plan for your life. And when it's time to sing the Psalm, join in with your whole heart. Even if you don't know all the words, let the music lift you up and remind you of how much God loves you. The Liturgy of the Word is an amazing opportunity to connect with God, learn from Him, and become a stronger part of His family.

The Gospel: Learning from Jesus' Words

The Gospel is always the highlight of the Liturgy of the Word. It's like the main event of the whole Bible! When the priest or deacon gets ready to read the Gospel, we all stand up as a sign of respect. It's our way of saying, "Hey, this is really important!" And it is, because the Gospel is where we hear directly from Jesus. It's like getting a letter or a message from your best friend or someone you really admire. Wouldn't you want to pay attention to every word they say?

But what is the Gospel exactly? The Gospel is made up of stories and teachings from Matthew, Mark, Luke, and John, who were the closest followers of Jesus. These four books are called the Gospels because they tell the "good news" of Jesus' life, death, and resurrection. Jesus came to earth to show us how to love, how to forgive, and how to live in a way that brings us closer to God.

Every time we read the Gospel, we're hearing the good news about God's love for us. The Gospel shows us that Jesus loves us so much that He was willing to sacrifice His life to save us. It's all about the love of God and how He wants us to love one another. Jesus taught His followers to love our neighbors, forgive those who hurt us, and care for the poor and the needy.

The Gospel is always something we should listen to carefully because it gives us a clear idea of how to live as Christians. Jesus' words are not just stories from the past; they are a guide to help us today. Imagine Jesus is right there with you, teaching you how to be a better person. That's what the Gospel is doing, it's showing you the way to live in God's love.

One of the coolest things about the Gospel is that it can speak to us no matter what we're going through. Whether you're feeling happy or sad, angry or peaceful, Jesus' words have something important for you to hear. If you're struggling with something at school or at home, Jesus' teachings on forgiveness or kindness can help you find a solution. If you're feeling confused or lost, the Gospel helps remind you that God is always with you and that He loves you no matter what.

After the Gospel is read, the priest or deacon says, "The Gospel of the Lord," and we all respond, "Praise to You, Lord Jesus Christ." This is our way of saying, "Thank You, Jesus, for teaching us! We're ready to live by Your words."

After the Gospel, we move to the homily, which is the priest or deacon's chance to explain the message of the Gospel and make it clear for us. The homily is like a lesson or a mini-sermon that helps us understand what we just heard. It's a chance for the priest to talk to us about how we can live out the teachings of Jesus in our daily lives. It's not just a lecture or a speech, it's a conversation between the priest and the congregation, helping us all grow in our faith.

During the homily, the priest will often break down the story or teaching from the Gospel and show us how it connects to our lives. For example, if the Gospel reading is about loving our neighbors, the priest might talk about how we can show love to the people around us, even when it's hard. He might share a story from his own life or from the lives of others to help us understand how to live out the message of the Gospel.

The homily is not just for adults—it's for everyone, no matter how old you are. The priest will often use examples and stories that make it easy for you to understand. He wants you to hear the message of Jesus and think about how it applies to your life. Maybe you've been having trouble getting along with a sibling, or you've been feeling discouraged about school. The homily can help you think about how Jesus' teachings can help you with those problems. The priest helps us see that the Gospel isn't just a book from long ago—it's a guide for today, for how we can make the world a better place by following Jesus' example.

Sometimes, the priest will ask us questions during the homily, or he might make us think about how we can do something better in our lives. It's like when a teacher asks you, "How would you handle this situation?" or "What would you do if…?" The priest does the same thing in the homily to get us thinking about how we can live out God's Word.

The homily isn't just about hearing words—it's about applying those words to our lives. It's like getting a set of instructions for building a better relationship with God and others. After hearing the homily, you might think about it for the rest of the day and try to put it into action. Maybe the priest talked about being kind to your friends, or how you can help others at school. These little reminders can make a huge difference in how you live your life and how you show God's love to the world.

Why the Gospel and Homily Matter

You might be wondering why the Gospel and homily are such big parts of Mass. After all, you could just listen to the priest say prayers, and that would be good enough, right? But the Gospel and the homily are important because they help us understand who God is and what He wants for us. The Gospel is God speaking to us directly, and the homily is how we take those words and apply them to our lives.

God wants us to hear His voice, not just in the Bible, but also in our daily lives. By listening to the Gospel and reflecting on the homily, we can learn how to become better people and how to grow closer to God. The Gospel reminds us that we're not just here on earth to live for ourselves—we're here to love others and share God's love with the world.

Another important part of the Gospel and homily is that they help us stay connected to God. Every time we hear the Gospel, we're reminded of the love God has for us, and how He wants us to love others. The homily helps us understand how we can live out that love in our everyday lives. It's like getting a weekly reminder to keep loving, keep forgiving, and keep growing in faith.

Finally, the Gospel and the homily make Mass come alive. Without them, Mass would be a lot of prayers and songs, but the Gospel and the homily give us the meat of Mass—the lessons we need to live a life full of God's love and purpose. So when you're listening to the Gospel or paying attention to the homily, remember: this is God speaking directly to you. It's your chance to learn more about who Jesus is and how you can follow Him in everything you do.

The next time you're at Mass, pay attention during the Gospel and the homily. Think about how the stories and teachings can help you live out God's Word in your life. Whether it's something big, like learning to forgive, or something small, like being kind to someone at school, the Gospel and homily are moments for you to hear God's voice and think about how you can make the world a little bit brighter with His love.

Chapter 6

Liturgy of the Eucharist

The Liturgy of the Eucharist is one of the most important and sacred parts of Mass. This is when we get to receive Holy Communion, which is when we receive Jesus Himself in the form of bread and wine. It's a beautiful, mysterious, and deeply meaningful moment, and it all starts with the Presentation of the Gifts and leads into the Consecration. Let's take a closer look at these two parts of the Liturgy of the Eucharist, because they help us prepare for the most amazing moment of Mass: receiving Jesus.

Getting Ready for Communion: Presentation of the Gifts

The Presentation of the Gifts is like the preparation for the most special meal ever! Before we receive Communion, there are some important things that happen on the altar. The gifts that are presented during Mass are the bread and wine. These gifts are brought up to the altar by the people in the congregation—usually by the altar servers or some members of the church—and they represent the things we offer to God. The bread and wine are simple gifts, but they become something so much more during Mass. These are the gifts that are going to be changed into the body and blood of Jesus during the Consecration.

But the Presentation of the Gifts is more than just handing over the bread and wine. It's a moment for all of us to think about what we are offering to God. The bread and wine represent our lives, too. Just like how we give the bread and wine to God, we also give God our hearts, our hopes, our prayers, and our dreams. The gifts are symbolic of everything we want to offer to God: our love, our thanks, and our desire to grow closer to Him.

During this part of the Mass, the priest also invites us to offer a prayer along with the gifts. As the bread and wine are placed on the altar, the priest says, "Blessed are You, Lord God of all creation, for through Your goodness we have received the bread we offer You…" It's like the priest is saying, "Thank You, God, for the things we have, and we offer them back to You." This moment is a beautiful reminder that everything we have is a gift from God, and we give it back to Him with gratitude.

When the gifts are placed on the altar, it's a symbol of our willingness to share with God what we have. It's not just about the bread and wine; it's about offering our hearts, our time, and our love. Everything we have comes from God, so when we offer these gifts, we're saying, "God, here's what I have. I give it to You." It's like when you give a gift to a friend or family member—you offer something with love and care, and that's what we're doing with God.

After the gifts are presented, the priest says another prayer, asking God to accept these gifts and make them holy. This prayer gets us ready for the next part of the Liturgy of the Eucharist, when the bread and wine will be transformed into the body and blood of Jesus. It's a way of saying, "We're ready, God. We've given You our hearts and lives. Now, help us receive You fully."

Jesus' Special Prayer: The Consecration

Now comes the most amazing part of the Liturgy of the Eucharist: the Consecration. The Consecration is when the bread and wine are changed into the body and blood of Jesus. It happens when the priest speaks the very same words that Jesus said at the Last Supper: "This is My body... This is My blood."

Before this moment, the bread and wine are just ordinary things that we use for the meal. But once the priest says the words of the Consecration, something amazing happens. The bread and wine are no longer just bread and wine—they are truly the body and blood of Jesus. It's a mystery because even though we can't see the bread and wine change, we believe with all our hearts that Jesus is really present in the Eucharist.

During the Consecration, the priest holds up the bread and says, "This is My body, which will be given up for you." When he says this, we're reminded of what Jesus did for us on the cross. He gave His body to save us. And now, every time we celebrate Mass, Jesus gives Himself to us in the Eucharist, offering us His love and forgiveness. The priest then holds up the chalice (the cup with wine), saying, "This is the blood of the new and eternal covenant, which will be poured out for you and for many for the forgiveness of sins." Jesus poured out His blood for us on the cross to wash away our sins and make us one with Him.

This moment of Consecration is so special because it's when Jesus comes to us in a real way. The bread and wine become Jesus. They're no longer just symbols—they are Jesus Himself! And that's the greatest gift of all. When we receive Communion, we are receiving Jesus into our bodies and hearts, and that is a gift we can never fully understand. But we believe it because Jesus said it, and we trust that He is faithful to His promises.

You might wonder, "How can bread and wine turn into Jesus? How does that work?" The Eucharist is a mystery, but it's a mystery that we believe in because Jesus told us it would happen. The Real Presence of Jesus in the Eucharist is one of the greatest miracles of our faith. Every time you receive Communion, you are receiving God's love in the most powerful way. It's like a big hug from God, reminding you that He is with you always.

After the Consecration, we say a prayer called the Mystery of Faith, where we proclaim that Jesus has died, risen, and will come again. This is a reminder that the Eucharist is not just about the past—it's about the present and the future, too. By receiving the Eucharist, we're uniting ourselves with the whole Church, not just in the here and now, but in the promise of eternal life with Jesus. It's a beautiful thing to remember, especially when we receive Jesus in Communion.

Why the Eucharist Matters

The Liturgy of the Eucharist is the heart of the Mass because it's when we get to receive Jesus in a way that is truly real. When we take the bread and wine that have become His body and blood, we are joining with Jesus in a deep, mysterious way. The Eucharist is not just a symbol of Jesus—it's Jesus Himself, offering us His love and presence.

In the Eucharist, Jesus gives us the strength to live as His followers. It's like eating food to fuel your body; the Eucharist nourishes our souls. By receiving Jesus, we are filled with the strength we need to face the challenges of the week ahead. It's like a spiritual recharge that helps us live better lives, follow Jesus more closely, and share His love with others.

The Eucharist also reminds us that we are not alone. We are part of a family—the Church—and when we receive Communion, we're united with all the people who love Jesus, no matter where they are in the world. The Eucharist is a reminder that we are all connected to one another through God's love. It's like being part of a big team, with Jesus as our coach, guiding us and helping us.

Receiving the Eucharist also teaches us to love. Jesus gave His body and blood for us because He loves us so much. When we receive Him in the Eucharist, we are called to share that love with others. The Eucharist is a reminder that love is at the heart of everything we do, and when we live with love, we are living the way Jesus wants us to live.

As you continue to celebrate Mass, always remember how special the Eucharist is. Every time you receive Communion, you're receiving Jesus—God's love, right into your heart. The Presentation of the Gifts and the Consecration are beautiful moments that help us prepare for this amazing gift. The Eucharist is not just a part of Mass—it's the center of it all, because it's where we meet Jesus in the most real way. So, next time you receive Communion, remember: you are receiving God's greatest gift, and that's something to be incredibly thankful for!

Mass is a time for us to be with God, to talk to Him, and to listen to what He has to say. One of the most beautiful and powerful parts of the Liturgy of the Eucharist happens when we all come together to pray, share peace, and ask God for help. It's a time when we really feel like we're part of God's family, not just by sitting in the same room, but by sharing in His love and connecting with each other. In this chapter, we're going to talk about two special moments in Mass: Saying the Lord's Prayer and Sharing the Peace and Saying the Lamb of God. These moments help us talk to God, ask for His help, and spread love and peace to everyone around us.

Talking to God: Saying the Lord's Prayer

One of the most famous prayers that we say during Mass is the Lord's Prayer, also known as the Our Father. This prayer was taught to us by Jesus Himself when His disciples asked Him how they should pray. Jesus didn't just say, "Pray however you want." Instead, He gave them a special prayer that covers everything we need to talk to God about. And now, every time we gather for Mass, we get to say this prayer together. It's a chance to speak to God, ask for His help, and remind ourselves that we are His children.

The Lord's Prayer starts with the words, "Our Father, who art in heaven." Right away, this tells us something really important. When we pray this, we are addressing God as our Father. This isn't just a distant ruler we're talking to—this is God who loves us, cares for us, and wants to help us. It's like calling your parent or a loving adult "Mom" or "Dad." God is not far away and disconnected; He's close and wants to have a personal relationship with us.

The next part of the prayer says, "Hallowed be Thy name," which means, "We honor Your name, God, and we want to keep it holy." This reminds us that God is holy and deserves our respect. We show respect to God through our actions and words, and the Lord's Prayer helps us remember how important He is in our lives.

The prayer then goes on to say, "Thy kingdom come, Thy will be done, on earth as it is in heaven." This is a way of asking God to bring His kingdom of love and peace to the world. It's like saying, "God, we want Your goodness to fill the earth, just like it does in heaven." We are asking God to help us live the way He wants us to live, with kindness, love, and respect for one another.

Next, the prayer asks God to "give us this day our daily bread." This is a request for God to take care of our needs—physically, emotionally, and spiritually. We're saying, "God, give us what we need today to get through life and to help others." In the Eucharist, the bread we receive is Jesus, the Bread of Life, so we're asking God to provide for us and help us grow closer to Him each day.

Then, we say, "And forgive us our trespasses, as we forgive those who trespass against us." This part of the prayer is important because it reminds us that forgiveness is a key part of being Christian. When we ask God to forgive us, we also promise to forgive others who may have hurt us. Forgiveness is hard sometimes, but this part of the prayer helps us remember that God forgives us, and we need to do the same for others.

The prayer continues with, "And lead us not into temptation, but deliver us from evil." We're asking God to help us make good choices and protect us from things that can lead us away from His love. It's a request for strength in difficult situations and a reminder that God is with us, keeping us safe from harm.

Finally, we end the prayer with "Amen," which means "So be it" or "Yes, I believe." When we say Amen, we're saying, "God, we trust You, and we believe in everything we just prayed."

The Lord's Prayer is so powerful because it covers everything we need in our relationship with God. It helps us pray for ourselves, for others, and for the world. Saying this prayer together at Mass is a beautiful reminder that we are all God's family, and we share the same needs, hopes, and dreams.

Peace and Harmony: Sharing the Peace and Saying the Lamb of God

After saying the Lord's Prayer, it's time for another special moment in Mass: sharing the peace and saying the Lamb of God. These parts of Mass help us remember that Mass isn't just about us—it's about being part of the whole Christian family and sharing love and peace with everyone around us. Let's look at what these moments mean and why they're so important.

Sharing the Peace

Right after we say the Lord's Prayer, the priest says, "The peace of the Lord be with you always," and we respond, "And with your spirit." This is a reminder that God's peace is with us. Then, the priest invites us to share that peace with the people around us. We do this by shaking hands or offering a simple "peace be with you" to those sitting next to us.

Sharing the peace is an important part of Mass because it reminds us that God's love isn't just for us individually, but for the whole world. It's also a way of showing that we are all united in love and faith. When we offer peace to others, we are telling them, "I care about you," and "I want you to experience God's love, too." It's a beautiful moment where we acknowledge that we are all connected by God's love, and we want to spread that peace everywhere we go.

Sometimes, it's easy to forget about the people around us, especially if we're feeling shy or distracted. But sharing the peace is a way to remind us that we are not alone in our faith. The peace we offer is a way of saying, "I'm here for you," and "I want you to feel God's presence, just like I do." It's like giving someone a hug or a kind word. When we share peace, we're showing kindness, and that's exactly what Jesus would want us to do.

Saying the Lamb of God

After we share the peace, we move on to saying the Lamb of God. This is a prayer where we call Jesus the "Lamb of God," and we ask Him to take away our sins and grant us peace. The words go like this: "Lamb of God, You take away the sins of the world, have mercy on us. Lamb of God, You take away the sins of the world, have mercy on us. Lamb of God, You take away the sins of the world, grant us peace."

The title "Lamb of God" is a reminder of what Jesus did for us. In the Old Testament, people would offer a lamb as a sacrifice to ask for forgiveness. But Jesus is the perfect Lamb—He gave His life for all of us so that we could be forgiven for our sins. When we say this prayer, we are asking Jesus to forgive us and to fill us with His peace. We acknowledge that Jesus is the sacrifice that takes away our sins and brings us back into a good relationship with God.

The "Lamb of God" prayer also helps us prepare for the most special moment in Mass: receiving Holy Communion. When we receive Communion, we are receiving the body and blood of the Lamb of God, who takes away our sins and fills us with His love and grace. Saying the Lamb of God prayer is a way of preparing our hearts for this amazing moment, where we get to meet Jesus face to face, in the form of the Eucharist.

Why These Moments Matter

The Lord's Prayer, sharing the peace, and saying the Lamb of God are not just things we do to fill time during Mass. They are all deeply meaningful actions that help us connect with God and with each other. The Lord's Prayer teaches us how to speak to God and ask for His love and help. Sharing the peace reminds us that we are all part of one big Christian family, united in love. And the Lamb of God prayer helps us prepare to receive Jesus and reminds us of the sacrifice He made for us.

When we say these prayers and share the peace, we are not just going through the motions. We are actively participating in Mass and showing God that we want to be close to Him, share His love with others, and be filled with His peace. These moments help us grow in faith and help us live out God's love in the world.

Next time you're at Mass, remember how special it is to say the Lord's Prayer with everyone around you, share the peace with those beside you, and prepare your heart to receive Jesus in the Eucharist through the Lamb of God. Each of these moments is a beautiful reminder of the love, peace, and forgiveness that Jesus offers to each one of us.

Receiving Communion: How We Get Jesus into Our Hearts

Have you ever been excited to receive a gift? Maybe it's your birthday or Christmas, and you're eager to open that special present. The feeling of receiving something so amazing and important is a little like what happens when we receive Communion at Mass. But instead of a wrapped-up present, we're receiving Jesus Himself, and it's the best gift ever! Communion is when we receive Jesus in the form of bread and wine. But how does that work, and why is it such a big deal? Let's explore what Communion is all about and how it brings Jesus into our hearts in a powerful way.

First things first—what exactly is Communion? Communion is when we receive the body and blood of Jesus during Mass. But it's not like eating a regular piece of bread or drinking a glass of wine. Communion is much more special than that. When we receive Communion, the bread and wine are changed into the real presence of Jesus. This means that, even though the bread and wine still look the same, they are now truly the body and blood of Jesus. It's a mystery, but it's a beautiful mystery that shows us how much God loves us and wants to be close to us.

The moment when we receive Communion is called the Eucharist, which comes from a word that means "thanksgiving." It's a way for us to thank God for everything He has done for us, especially for sending Jesus to be with us. When we take Communion, we're saying, "Thank You, Jesus, for coming into my life and giving me Your love." It's the ultimate way to connect with Jesus and feel His love in our hearts.

Why Do We Receive Communion?

You might be wondering, "Why do we need Communion in the first place?" Great question! We receive Communion because Jesus wants to be with us. When Jesus was with His friends at the Last Supper, He told them to "do this in memory of me" (Luke 22:19). He wanted them to remember Him and keep that close connection with Him, even after He returned to Heaven. So, at Mass, we come together to celebrate Jesus' sacrifice and receive Him into our lives. Communion is how we stay close to Jesus and make sure His love stays alive in our hearts.

Communion is also a way for us to feel God's presence in a very real and powerful way. Even though we can't see Jesus with our eyes like the disciples did, He's still present in the Eucharist. This is why we treat Communion with so much respect and reverence—because we're receiving Jesus Himself into our hearts.

Receiving Communion is a way to remember that we are part of God's family. We come together as a community to celebrate this special moment. When we eat the body and blood of Jesus, we're not just doing it by ourselves; we're doing it with everyone at Mass, all around the world, and even across time. It's like a big family meal, where we're united with other Christians who believe in Jesus.

How Do We Receive Communion?

When it's time to receive Communion, we walk up to the altar, just like the rest of the congregation. If you're receiving the host (the bread), the priest or Eucharistic minister will say, "The Body of Christ," and you'll respond, "Amen." Saying "Amen" is like saying, "Yes, I believe this is

Jesus, and I'm ready to receive Him into my heart." Then, you take the host and eat it right there. It's a moment when you're meeting Jesus in the most personal way—by receiving Him into your own body.

Sometimes, if you're receiving from the chalice (the wine), the Eucharistic minister will say, "The Blood of Christ," and you'll respond with the same "Amen." You can drink the wine or, if you prefer, choose to receive just the host. Both are equally Jesus—the bread and wine are the body and blood of Christ, and each part is fully Him.

After receiving Communion, you may walk back to your seat and take a moment to reflect. It's a good time to thank Jesus for coming into your heart and ask Him to help you live His love in the world. You can say a quick prayer in your heart, like, "Thank You, Jesus, for being with me. Help me to love others like You love me."

After you receive Communion, you might feel different. It's normal! You've just received the most amazing gift possible—Jesus. Sometimes, you might feel peaceful and calm, or maybe you feel energized and ready to live your life better. Whatever you're feeling, just know that Jesus is with you, and He's always there to help you.

In some churches, there's a moment of silent prayer after Communion. This is a time to be quiet and reflect on the amazing thing that just happened. You've just received God's love in a very real way, and it's a chance to thank Him for everything He's done for you.

The Importance of Communion in Our Lives

Now that you know what Communion is and how we receive it, let's talk about why it's so important for your life. Communion isn't just something you do once—it's something you can keep in your heart every day. When you receive Communion, it's like putting on a new pair of glasses that help you see the world through God's eyes. You get to experience life with God's love guiding you.

Communion helps us grow stronger in our faith. It's like getting recharged after a long day or a tough week. When we receive Jesus in the Eucharist, we're reminded that we don't have to go through life alone. God is always with us, walking beside us, helping us in every situation.

Think about how much your friends and family mean to you. When you spend time with them, you grow closer to them, right? The same is true with God. The more time you spend with Him—especially when you receive Communion—the stronger your relationship with Him becomes. You get to know God better and better. You learn what He wants for your life, and you get better at loving others the way He loves you.

When you receive Communion, it's not just about eating bread or drinking wine—it's about living out the love you've just received. Communion is a calling. It's a way of saying, "Jesus, I want to follow You and share Your love with others." So, after Mass, go out and live the love you just received. Show kindness, forgive others, be patient, and share God's love in everything you do.

It's not always easy, but with Jesus in your heart, you can do anything. Communion gives you the strength to be the best version of yourself, helping others and being a light in the world. Every time you receive Communion, you're saying, "I want to live like Jesus, and I want His love to shine through me."

Receiving Communion is one of the most amazing experiences in Mass. It's the moment when Jesus comes into your heart in a very real way. Through the bread and wine, Jesus gives you Himself—His love, His strength, and His grace. It's the greatest gift, and it helps you grow closer to God. So, the next time you go to Mass and receive Communion, remember just how special it is. You are receiving the love of God, and that's something you can carry with you all week long.

Chapter 7

The Liturgy of the Eucharist

Mass is full of important moments that help us grow closer to God, but one of the most special parts of the Mass is the Eucharistic Prayer. This prayer happens right before we receive Holy Communion, and it's when we ask God to make the bread and wine into the Body and Blood of Jesus. The Eucharistic Prayer is a long and beautiful prayer, and it's the moment when we really experience God's love in a powerful way. So, let's talk about the big prayers of the Mass and how the Eucharistic Prayer helps us understand God's love even better.

Praying Together: The Big Prayers of the Mass

The Eucharistic Prayer is actually made up of a series of big prayers that are said together by the priest and the congregation. It's like a conversation between the priest, the Church, and God. The priest leads the prayer, but we all join in by saying Amen at different points, showing that we believe in what's being said. Think of it like when you're in a group and everyone says something together. When everyone says "Amen," it's like saying, "Yes, we believe this, and we agree!"

The Eucharistic Prayer starts with a special greeting: "The Lord be with you," and the congregation responds, "And with your spirit." This is a way of acknowledging that God is with us and that we are all ready to pray together. The priest then says, "Lift up your hearts," and we respond, "We lift them up to the Lord." This is a reminder that we're not just going through the motions; we're offering our hearts and our prayers to God.

Next, the priest says, "Let us give thanks to the Lord our God," and we respond, "It is right and just." This is a way of acknowledging that it is good and right for us to give thanks to God for everything He has done for us. The Eucharistic Prayer is all about thanksgiving—thanking God for sending Jesus to save us and for giving us the gift of the Eucharist. We are celebrating all the wonderful things God has done, and we do this through prayer and praise.

Easy Ways to Understand the Eucharistic Prayers

The Eucharistic Prayer is full of beautiful words that can be a little hard to understand at first, but they all have a special meaning. Let's break down some of the key parts of the Eucharistic Prayer to make it easier for you to understand what's going on.

The Preface: Thanking God for Everything

Before the priest begins the prayer that transforms the bread and wine into the Body and Blood of Jesus, he says what is called the Preface. The Preface is the part of the prayer where the priest thanks God for all the amazing things He has done. It's like saying, "Thank you, God, for everything you've given us." The priest talks about how God created the world, how He sent Jesus to show us His love, and how Jesus died and rose again to save us. The Preface sets the stage for everything that follows in the Eucharistic Prayer. It's a way to get us in the right mindset of gratitude and awe before we get to the part where we celebrate the Eucharist.

The Holy, Holy, Holy: Praising God

One of the most famous parts of the Eucharistic Prayer is the Holy, Holy, Holy. The priest starts saying, "Holy, Holy, Holy, Lord God of hosts," and we all join in by singing or saying, "Hosanna in the highest." This part of the prayer comes directly from the Bible (from the book of Isaiah), and it's a way of praising God for His greatness. The angels in heaven praise God this way, and now we are joining them in saying how amazing God is.

The Holy, Holy, Holy is our way of showing God how much we love Him and how much we want to praise Him for being so great. It's like when you're cheering for your favorite team or shouting out, "I love you!" to someone who means a lot to you. We are telling God, "You are the best, and we are so thankful for You."

The Epiclesis: Asking the Holy Spirit to Help Us

After the Holy, Holy, Holy, we move into a part of the Eucharistic Prayer called the Epiclesis. This is when the priest asks the Holy Spirit to come down upon the bread and wine and make them the Body and Blood of Jesus. It's like asking the Holy Spirit to work a miracle. The priest says, "Send Your Spirit upon these gifts to make them holy." At this moment, the bread and wine are changed, and they become Jesus. The Epiclesis is when we ask the Holy Spirit to help make this miracle happen, and it's a reminder that it's not just the priest's words that make the bread and wine holy—it's God's power through the Holy Spirit.

The Institution Narrative: Jesus' Words

Now, we get to the part of the Eucharistic Prayer where we remember what Jesus did at the Last Supper. The priest speaks the words that Jesus said: "Take this, all of you, and eat of it. This is My Body, which will be given up for you." Then, he does the same with the wine, saying, "This is the chalice of My Blood, the Blood of the new and eternal covenant." This part is called the Institution Narrative because it tells the story of when Jesus first gave us the Eucharist. Jesus told His disciples that this bread and wine were no longer just regular food and drink—they were His Body and Blood, given for us.

This is the moment when the bread and wine are transformed into the Body and Blood of Jesus. Even though the bread and wine still look the same, they are now truly Jesus. This moment is the most special part of the Eucharistic Prayer because we are participating in the same act that Jesus did with His disciples. Every time we go to Mass, we're experiencing this sacred moment where Jesus gives Himself to us, just like He did at the Last Supper.

The Memorial Acclamation: Remembering Jesus

After the priest says the words of Jesus, we respond with the Memorial Acclamation. This is a part of the prayer where we say, "When we eat this bread and drink this cup, we proclaim Your death, O Lord, until You come again." This is our way of remembering Jesus' death and resurrection and also of looking forward to the time when He will return. The Memorial Acclamation is like a promise we make: we believe that Jesus died for us, He rose again, and He will come back to make all things new. It's our way of saying, "Yes, Jesus, we believe in You, and we remember what You did for us."

The Eucharistic Prayer is not just a long prayer full of fancy words—it's a beautiful conversation with God. The priest leads us in this prayer, but we all join in by saying "Amen" and praying together. This prayer reminds us that the Eucharist is all about thanksgiving—thanking God for sending us Jesus and for the miracle of the Eucharist. It also helps us remember the great sacrifice that Jesus made for us and how He is still with us today in the Eucharist.

When you hear the words of the Eucharistic Prayer, think of them as God's special way of giving us love and grace. The Eucharistic Prayer is when we thank God, remember Jesus' sacrifice, and ask the Holy Spirit to help us experience that love in a real way. It's a powerful prayer that unites us with God and with everyone in the Church, making us stronger in our faith.

The next time you're at Mass and the Eucharistic Prayer is being said, remember that you are part of something much bigger than yourself. It's not just the priest praying—it's all of us coming together to thank God and ask for His help. The Eucharistic Prayer is a special moment where God's love comes alive, and we are invited to join in this sacred conversation. When we receive Communion, we're receiving the Body and Blood of Jesus, and that's a huge gift. The Eucharistic Prayer helps us prepare our hearts for this moment and reminds us of God's incredible love for each one of us.

Chapter 8

Concluding Rites

Mass is such a special time. It's a chance to gather with others, hear God's Word, sing songs of praise, and receive Jesus in the Eucharist. But just like how a party or a fun event has to end, Mass has a conclusion too. The Concluding Rites are the final part of Mass, and they help us wrap up our time together in a way that leaves us feeling ready to go out into the world and share God's love. Let's dive into the Concluding Rites and see how we say goodbye to God, receive His final blessings, and leave Mass with Jesus in our hearts.

Getting Ready to Go: Announcements

After receiving Communion and hearing the Eucharistic Prayer, it might feel like Mass is over, but there are still a few important things to do before we finish. The first thing that happens during the Concluding Rites is the announcements. Now, you might be thinking, "Why do we have announcements at the end of Mass?" It's not like the priest is going to start talking about homework or what's for lunch! Announcements at Mass are there to help us stay connected to the Church and the community.

For example, the priest might announce upcoming events like a parish picnic, a special Mass for a holy day, or an opportunity to help others in need. These announcements help us stay involved and remember that our relationship with God isn't just about what happens inside the church—it's also about what we do in the world around us.

In some ways, the announcements are a little bit like when your teacher or coach tells you what's coming up next. It's their way of saying, "Hey, now that we've done this great thing, here's what's next." It's a chance for the priest to share ways you can continue growing in your faith, participate in the life of the Church, or help others in the community.

Even though the announcements are short, they're important because they connect us with God's mission in the world. The Mass might be ending, but there's still more to do to share God's love and show His kindness. Announcements help us stay on track, encouraging us to live out the lessons we've learned in Mass once we leave the church.

Saying Goodbye: Final Blessing and Dismissal

Now that we've heard the announcements, it's time for the Final Blessing. This is the priest's way of sending us out into the world with God's love and peace. When the priest says, "The Lord be with you," and we respond, "And with your spirit," it's like a little reminder that God is always with us, no matter where we go. The Final Blessing is a time to pause and think about how we're going to carry the love and peace we've received at Mass with us throughout the week.

The priest then says a special prayer to bless us, asking God to keep us safe, strong, and filled with His love. It's like a spiritual boost that helps us get ready to face the challenges and joys of the week. The Final Blessing is like a loving "goodbye" from God. Even though Mass is ending, God is telling us that He is going with us, and He will always be there to help us.

One of the most important things about the Final Blessing is that it reminds us of our mission. When we leave the church, we're not just going back to regular life. We're going out as God's children, ready to share His love with everyone we meet. Whether we're at school, at home, with friends, or in our community, the Final Blessing helps us remember that we are always representing God's love. It's like when you leave a fun event, and you know you have to share the joy with others. The Final Blessing sends us out to do that, but with God's help and strength.

After the priest gives the Final Blessing, he says, "Go in peace, glorifying the Lord by your life." This is where the Mass ends, but it's not really a "goodbye" in the traditional sense. It's more of a "go and do great things" kind of send-off. When the priest says this, he's reminding us that our job isn't done once we leave the church. Instead, we're being sent out to carry the message of love, kindness, and peace into the world. It's like being given a mission: Go out and make the world a better place by living like Jesus did. We're not just listening to God's Word and receiving Jesus in Communion for ourselves; we're getting ready to share everything we've learned with others.

Walking Out: Leaving Mass with Jesus in Our Hearts

Now comes the final step—the dismissal. After the Final Blessing, we walk out of the church, but we don't leave empty-handed. We leave with Jesus in our hearts, and that's the most important thing of all. When we receive Communion, it's not just a one-time thing. The love and strength we receive from Jesus stay with us, helping us live our lives in a way that reflects His love and kindness.

Think of it like this: imagine you've just had an amazing meal at a friend's house, and when it's time to go, they send you home with some leftovers. You're not going home hungry because you've got a little extra to take with you! In a similar way, when we leave Mass, we're not leaving empty. We're taking Jesus' love and peace with us. We've been spiritually fed, and now we get to go out and share that nourishment with the world. Whether it's being kind to a friend, helping a sibling, or simply showing patience, every little thing we do can be a way to live out the love of Jesus we've received.

Walking out of Mass is like stepping into the world with Jesus by our side. We're not alone. The love we received in the Eucharist and the blessings we've received at Mass are meant to help us live better lives. As we leave, we're called to bring that love into every part of our day. The dismissal reminds us that the Mass isn't just about what happens inside the church—it's about how we live our faith every single day. We are sent out to be witnesses to the world, showing others the love of God through our actions.

The Concluding Rites might seem like the final part of Mass, but they're actually some of the most important moments because they help us apply what we've learned during Mass to our lives. The announcements help us stay connected to the Church and remind us of ways we can serve God and others. The Final Blessing helps us feel empowered and ready to face the week ahead with God's peace and strength. And the dismissal sends us out to be the hands and feet of Jesus, sharing His love in everything we do.

Every part of the Concluding Rites reminds us that Mass doesn't end when we leave the church. In fact, it's only just beginning. We're being sent out to live the love we've received, and we're doing that with Jesus by our side. So, when you walk out of Mass next time, remember that you're walking out with Jesus in your heart, ready to share that love with everyone you meet.

Mass may have ended, but the journey doesn't stop there. We're called to live out everything we've received and share God's peace and love with the world. Just like a light shining in the darkness, your actions and choices can make a big difference in the world around you. And with Jesus in your heart, there's no limit to the good you can do.

Chapter 9

All the People's Parts in Order

Going to Mass is an exciting time where you get to learn, sing, and spend time with God. But sometimes, all the prayers and movements during Mass can feel a bit confusing. Don't worry though! In this chapter, we're going to break down what we say during Mass, and when we need to stand, sit, and kneel. It'll help you feel more confident and make Mass feel like a fun, easy experience.

What We Say

When you're at Mass, you'll notice that the priest doesn't say everything alone. There are many parts of the Mass where you get to join in with your voice, too! Mass is like a conversation between you, the priest, and God. Sometimes you'll say prayers out loud with everyone, sometimes you'll respond to the priest, and sometimes you'll say prayers silently in your heart. Knowing what to say will help you feel more involved and make Mass even more special!

Here's a quick-reference guide to all the responses and prayers you'll say during Mass:

1. The Opening Greeting

When the priest says, "The Lord be with you," you reply, "And with your spirit." This is like saying, "Hello!" to God at the beginning of Mass. It's a nice way to start Mass with respect and a reminder that God is with us.

2. The Gloria

After the opening greeting, we all say the Gloria. It's a joyful prayer where we praise God. It goes like this:

"Glory to God in the highest, and on earth peace to people of good will. We praise You, we bless You, we adore You, we glorify You, we give You thanks for Your great glory, Lord God, Heavenly King, O God, Almighty Father."

It might sound a little long, but it's a song of joy and love for God.

3. The Nicene Creed or Apostles' Creed

This prayer is when we remind ourselves what we believe in as Christians. It starts like this:

"We believe in one God, the Father Almighty, Maker of heaven and earth, of all things visible and invisible…"

It's a beautiful moment when everyone says together, "Yes, I believe in God." It's like saying, "I'm part of God's family."

4. The Lord's Prayer (Our Father)

When the priest invites everyone to pray the Our Father, you say this prayer with everyone. It's a prayer Jesus taught His disciples and it goes like this:

"Our Father, who art in heaven, hallowed be Thy name; Thy kingdom come; Thy will be done, on earth as it is in heaven. Give us this day our daily bread, and forgive us our trespasses, as we forgive those who trespass against us…"

This prayer is so important because it's like talking to God directly and asking Him for help in our lives.

5. The Sign of Peace

The priest says, "The peace of the Lord be with you always," and everyone replies, "And with your spirit." After that, you share the peace with people around you by shaking their hands or offering a smile. It's a way of sharing love and friendship with the people in your church family.

6. The Lamb of God

Before Communion, we pray the Lamb of God. It goes like this:

"Lamb of God, You take away the sins of the world, have mercy on us. Lamb of God, You take away the sins of the world, have mercy on us. Lamb of God, You take away the sins of the world, grant us peace."

We say this because Jesus is the Lamb of God, who takes away all our mistakes (sins) and helps us live with peace.

7. Communion Responses

When the priest or Eucharistic minister says, "The Body of Christ," you respond by saying, “Amen.” This shows that you believe that the bread is Jesus’ Body and that you are receiving Him into your heart. It’s like saying, “Yes, I accept Jesus’ love in my life.”

What to Do: When to Stand, Sit, and Kneel

During Mass, you’ll notice that people are standing, sitting, and kneeling at different times. These movements are part of how we show respect, focus on God, and participate in Mass. It can feel a little confusing at first, but don’t worry—we’re going to go through it all so you’ll know exactly what to do!

When to Stand: Showing Respect and Readiness

Standing is a way to show respect and readiness. When we stand at Mass, we’re showing God that we’re ready to listen, pray, and participate. Here’s when you should stand during Mass:

1. When the priest enters and during the entrance procession.

This is like standing to greet someone important when they walk into the room. The priest is coming to lead us in worship, so we stand to show respect and excitement for the start of Mass.

2. During the Gospel reading.

When the priest or deacon announces the Gospel, we stand. The Gospel is the most important part of the readings because it tells us about the life of Jesus. Standing shows that we respect these words and are ready to hear what Jesus has to say to us.

3. During prayers like the Nicene Creed and the Our Father.

We stand during the Creed because it’s a prayer where we declare our belief in God. Standing shows that we’re ready to proclaim what we believe. When we pray the Our Father, we stand to show that we’re talking directly to God as His children.

4. During the Eucharistic Prayer.

We stand during this part of Mass because we are about to receive the Body and Blood of Jesus. It’s a sign of respect for the great gift that we are about to receive.

When to Sit: Listening and Reflecting

Sitting is a way to get comfortable and focus on listening and reflecting. We sit when we're going to listen to readings from the Bible or when the priest is giving a homily (the talk or lesson). Sitting helps us pay attention to what is being said and think about how it applies to our lives.

1. During the First and Second Readings.

You'll sit during the First Reading and the Second Reading because these are parts of Mass where we listen to stories from the Bible. We sit to show that we are focused and ready to reflect on God's Word.

2. During the homily (priest's talk).

The priest gives a homily after the readings to help us understand what the Scriptures mean and how we can live them out in our lives. We sit to listen carefully to his message and think about how we can apply what he's saying.

When to Kneel: Showing Reverence and Prayer

Kneeling is one of the most important gestures we do at Mass. It shows reverence and humility. When we kneel, we are showing God how much we love Him and how much we respect His greatness. We also kneel to pray and focus our hearts on God.

1. During the Eucharistic Prayer.

We kneel when the priest is praying over the bread and wine to make them the Body and Blood of Jesus. This is the moment when the Real Presence of Jesus comes to us, and kneeling is a way of showing how special and sacred this moment is.

2. During the time right before Communion.

When the priest says, "Behold the Lamb of God," and the Lamb of God prayer is said, we kneel again. This is a time to reflect on the great gift we are about to receive in Communion and to prepare our hearts to welcome Jesus.

Why All the Movements Matter

You might wonder, "Why do we have to stand, sit, and kneel so many times during Mass?" The reason for all these movements is that they help us engage with God and show respect. Each movement has a special meaning:

- Standing shows we're ready to listen to God's Word and ready to receive His love.
- Sitting helps us focus on listening to the Bible readings and the priest's homily.
- Kneeling shows our love for God and prepares us to receive the Eucharist with reverence.

These movements help us participate in Mass not just with our voices, but also with our bodies. When we stand, sit, and kneel, we're expressing our feelings to God. We show respect when we stand and kneel, and we show attentiveness when we sit. All of these movements work together to make the Mass feel special and help us connect with God in different ways.

Why the Responses and Movements Help Us Stay Focused

At first, all the movements and prayers might seem a bit much, but they actually help us stay focused during Mass. They guide us through the different parts of Mass and keep us engaged with God. By saying the responses and following along with the movements, we are staying connected to the Mass and participating in a special way. You're not just sitting there; you're actively involved in talking to God, listening to His Word, and preparing your heart to receive Jesus in Communion.

The responses and movements at Mass help you feel part of the community, and they also help you remember that you're not alone. Everyone at Mass is there for the same purpose: to worship God and grow in love and faith. So when you stand, sit, kneel, and say the responses, you're joining in with everyone around you to create a space of love, respect, and prayer. It's like being part of a big, spiritual team, all working together to honor God.

Next time you're at Mass, remember what each movement and prayer means. Whether you're standing, sitting, or kneeling, you're participating in something really special. All the things we say and do in Mass help us connect with God and show Him our love and respect. Mass is an opportunity to grow closer to God, and knowing when and why we stand, sit, and kneel will help you make the most of this awesome time together!

Chapter 10

Common Prayers We Say

When we go to church or spend time in prayer, one of the best ways to talk to God is through prayers we know by heart. These are prayers that we've learned over time and are easy to say whenever we need them. In this chapter, we'll talk about three really important prayers that many people know well: Our Father, Hail Mary, and Glory Be. We'll also talk about the Saint Michael Prayer, which is a special prayer where we ask for help from God and His angels. Let's dive into these prayers and see what makes them so special!

Our Father, Hail Mary, and Glory Be: Prayers We Know By Heart

These three prayers are probably some of the first ones you learned when you were younger. You've heard them over and over again, and now, they're prayers that you can easily say whenever you need them. These prayers are powerful because they remind us of God's love, His guidance, and His care for us. Even though they're simple, they carry deep meaning and help us connect with God.

Our Father: The Perfect Prayer

The Our Father, also called the Lord's Prayer, is a prayer that Jesus taught His disciples. It's the perfect prayer because it covers everything we need when talking to God. Jesus didn't just teach this prayer for the people who were around Him back then—He wanted it to be passed down to everyone, including us today.

The Our Father starts with "Our Father, who art in heaven, hallowed be Thy name." This part reminds us that we're talking to God, our Father, who loves us more than anything. Saying "who art in heaven" helps us remember that God is not just any father; He's the one who created everything in the universe. The phrase "hallowed be Thy name" means we're saying God's name is holy, and we respect Him above all things.

Next, we pray, "Thy kingdom come, Thy will be done, on earth as it is in heaven." This part is like saying, "God, we want Your love and goodness to fill the world." We're asking God to bring His heavenly kingdom here on earth so that we can live in peace and love with each other, just like they do in heaven.

Then, we ask God, "Give us this day our daily bread." This part is a request for God to take care of us—not just with food, but with everything we need in life. Whether we need guidance, strength, or peace, we're asking God to provide us with what we need today. It's a reminder that we depend on God for everything, and He always gives us what's best for us.

We also say, "And forgive us our trespasses, as we forgive those who trespass against us." This is a big one! We're asking God to forgive us for our mistakes, just like we need to forgive others who might have hurt us. This part of the prayer teaches us the power of forgiveness—both asking for it and giving it. Forgiving others might not always be easy, but the Our Father helps us remember that God forgives us, and we should do the same for others.

We end the Our Father with, "And lead us not into temptation, but deliver us from evil." Here, we're asking God to help us stay strong and make good choices. We know that life can be hard, and sometimes it's tempting to do things that aren't right. But when we pray, "lead us not into temptation," we're asking God to protect us and help us live the way He wants us to.

Finally, we say "Amen," which means "Yes, I believe," and it's a way of saying, "God, I agree with everything we've just asked for." The Our Father is a powerful prayer because it brings us closer to God and helps us align our hearts with His will.

Hail Mary: A Prayer of Love for Mary

The Hail Mary is another prayer that you probably know by heart. This prayer is all about honoring Mary, the mother of Jesus, and asking for her help. Mary is a very special person because she was chosen by God to be the mother of Jesus, and she loves us just like a mother would.

The Hail Mary starts with "Hail Mary, full of grace, the Lord is with thee." These words are based on what the angel Gabriel said to Mary when he told her she was going to be the mother of Jesus. Saying this reminds us that Mary was chosen by God, and she's a beautiful example of faith, obedience, and love.

Next, we say, "Blessed art thou among women, and blessed is the fruit of thy womb, Jesus." This part honors Mary for being the mother of Jesus, who is the greatest gift the world has ever received. By saying this, we recognize how blessed Mary is to have been the mother of our Savior.

The final part of the prayer says, "Holy Mary, Mother of God, pray for us sinners, now and at the hour of our death." In this line, we're asking Mary to pray for us. We're asking her to intercede for us with God, just like a friend might pray for you when you're going through something difficult. Mary cares deeply about us and wants to help us, so we turn to her for her prayers and support.

The Hail Mary is a prayer of love and respect for Mary, and it helps us feel connected to her as our spiritual mother. She wants to lead us closer to her Son, Jesus, and help us grow in our faith.

Glory Be: Praising God

The Glory Be is a short prayer that helps us praise God for His greatness. It's also called the Doxology, and it's all about recognizing God's power and glory. The prayer goes, "Glory be to the Father, and to the Son, and to the Holy Spirit, as it was in the beginning, is now, and ever shall be, world without end. Amen."

When we say the Glory Be, we are praising God the Father, Jesus the Son, and the Holy Spirit—the three persons of the Holy Trinity. We are acknowledging that God is three in one: Father, Son, and Holy Spirit, and that He is with us forever. This prayer reminds us that God has always been, is, and will always be, and we give Him praise for His never-ending love and power.

Saint Michael Prayer: Asking for Help

Now let's talk about a special prayer called the Saint Michael Prayer. This prayer asks for help and protection from Saint Michael, the archangel. Archangels are powerful angels that help guide us and protect us from evil, and Saint Michael is one of the strongest and bravest angels of all. The Saint Michael Prayer is often said when we need extra help fighting against things that might tempt us or cause us to be afraid.

The prayer goes like this:

"Saint Michael the Archangel, defend us in battle. Be our protection against the wickedness and snares of the devil. May God rebuke him, we humbly pray; and do thou, O Prince of the Heavenly Host, by the power of God, cast into hell Satan and all the evil spirits who prowl about the world seeking the ruin of souls. Amen."

This prayer is like asking Saint Michael to be our protector and to help us stay strong when we face challenges or temptations. We are asking him to keep us safe from anything that might pull us away from God's love, and to fight against the devil and the evil that tries to harm us. It's a powerful prayer that helps us remember that God's angels are always there to help us stay safe and faithful to God.

Why These Prayers Matter

These prayers—Our Father, Hail Mary, Glory Be, and the Saint Michael Prayer—are important because they connect us to God, Mary, and the saints in a special way. They help us talk to God, ask for His help, and grow closer to Him. When you say these prayers, you're not just repeating words—you're connecting with God, expressing your faith, and seeking His guidance.

Having these prayers memorized means that you can say them whenever you need them. You can say the Our Father when you're feeling nervous or anxious, or the Hail Mary when you want to feel close to Mary. The Glory Be is a way to praise God anytime, and the Saint Michael Prayer is there to ask for protection whenever you need it. These prayers are like spiritual tools you can carry with you throughout your day, helping you stay connected to God no matter what's going on.

By saying these prayers regularly, you're building a strong relationship with God and His heavenly helpers. They remind you that you are never alone, and that God's love is always with you, guiding you, protecting you, and helping you grow in faith. So keep these prayers in your heart, and use them to talk to God anytime you need Him.

Act of Contrition: Saying Sorry to God

Sometimes, we make mistakes. Maybe we're mean to someone, say something unkind, or forget to do something important. Everyone makes mistakes—nobody's perfect—but the best way to make things right with God is by saying sorry. That's where the Act of Contrition comes in. This prayer is a simple way to tell God, "I'm sorry for my sins, and I want to do better."

The Act of Contrition is a prayer where we ask God to forgive us for the mistakes we've made, or as the prayer says, our "sins." It helps us remember that God is always ready to forgive us when we are truly sorry. When you say the Act of Contrition, you're not just saying, "Sorry," you're also promising to try harder next time and make better choices.

The prayer goes like this:

"My God, I am sorry for my sins with all my heart. In choosing to do wrong and failing to do good, I have sinned against You whom I should love above all things. I firmly intend, with Your help, to do penance, to sin no more, and to avoid whatever leads me to sin. Our Savior Jesus Christ suffered and died for us. In His name, my God, have mercy."

It might seem like a lot of words, but each part of the prayer has a special meaning. The first part, "I am sorry for my sins with all my heart," shows that we are really sorry for the wrong things we've done. We're not just saying sorry because we're caught or because we feel bad. We're saying sorry because we know that our actions have hurt God, and we want to fix that.

The next part says, "In choosing to do wrong and failing to do good, I have sinned against You." This part helps us recognize that our actions affect God and others. When we don't make the right choices, it hurts our relationship with God, and that's why we need to ask for forgiveness.

Then, we say, "I firmly intend, with Your help, to do penance, to sin no more, and to avoid whatever leads me to sin." This part is important because it shows that we want to do better. It's like saying, "I'm going to try harder next time, and I'm going to avoid the things that lead me to mess up." We're not just sorry for what we've done; we're making a plan to do better in the future. And we ask for God's help because we know we can't do it alone. God is always there to help us grow stronger and do better.

Lastly, we say, "Our Savior Jesus Christ suffered and died for us. In His name, my God, have mercy." This is a reminder that Jesus gave His life for us, and because of Him, we can be forgiven. Jesus' sacrifice on the cross made it possible for our sins to be forgiven, and this part of the prayer is a way to thank God for that amazing gift.

The Act of Contrition is a great prayer to say when you've done something wrong and want to make things right with God. It can also be said during Confession, when you're asking a priest to forgive your sins. But you don't need to wait until Confession to say it! You can say this prayer anytime you want to ask God for forgiveness and be honest with Him about the mistakes you've made. Saying the Act of Contrition helps you feel lighter, knowing that you're starting fresh with God's help.

How to Pray the Rosary: A Special Prayer We Do with Beads

The Rosary is another special prayer that helps you feel close to God and reflect on important moments in Jesus and Mary's lives. It's a meditative prayer, which means it helps you think deeply about God's love and the lessons Jesus taught us. You don't need to be in church to pray the Rosary—you can pray it anywhere, and it's a great way to focus your thoughts on God, especially when you're feeling distracted or need some peace.

The Rosary is prayed with a set of beads that help you keep track of your prayers. It might seem complicated at first, but once you get the hang of it, it becomes an easy and beautiful way to pray. Here's how to pray the Rosary step by step:

1. Start with the Cross.

Begin by holding the crucifix (the cross with Jesus on it) and say the Apostles' Creed. This is a prayer that tells us what we believe as Christians. It starts like this:

"I believe in God, the Father almighty, Creator of heaven and earth, and in Jesus Christ, His only Son, our Lord…"

This prayer is important because it reminds us of our faith and everything we believe about God, Jesus, and the Holy Spirit.

2. Say the Our Father.

Next, move to the first bead after the crucifix and say the Our Father. This is the prayer Jesus taught us, asking God to provide for us, forgive us, and help us live the way He wants us to.

3. Say three Hail Marys.

Next, on the next three beads, say three Hail Marys. These are prayers asking Mary, the mother of Jesus, to pray for us. Each Hail Mary is a way of honoring Mary and asking for her help in following Jesus.

4. Say the Glory Be.

After the three Hail Marys, say the Glory Be prayer, which praises God. The prayer goes:

"Glory be to the Father, and to the Son, and to the Holy Spirit, as it was in the beginning, is now, and ever shall be, world without end. Amen."

5. Start the First Mystery.

Now, you begin the first Mystery of the Rosary. There are five mysteries in the Rosary, each focusing on an important event in the lives of Jesus and Mary. These events are grouped into four categories:

- Joyful Mysteries (about the early life of Jesus)
- Sorrowful Mysteries (about Jesus' suffering and death)
- Glorious Mysteries (about Jesus' resurrection and glory)
- Luminous Mysteries (about the public ministry of Jesus)
- You'll meditate on the first mystery while you move to the next bead. For example, for the first Joyful Mystery, the Annunciation, you would think about the angel Gabriel visiting Mary and telling her she would become the mother of Jesus.

6. Pray one Our Father, ten Hail Marys, and one Glory Be.

For each mystery, you'll pray:

- One Our Father
- Ten Hail Marys
- One Glory Be
- As you do this, you'll be moving around the beads of the Rosary. The ten Hail Marys are said in a row as you meditate on the mystery.

7. Repeat for the Other Mysteries.

You'll repeat the same pattern for the next four mysteries. Once you've prayed the five mysteries, you've finished one set of the Rosary.

8. End with the Hail Holy Queen.

When you're finished with all the mysteries, you say the Hail Holy Queen, a prayer that asks Mary to be with you as you follow Jesus:

"Hail, Holy Queen, Mother of Mercy, our life, our sweetness, and our hope..."

The Rosary is a wonderful way to pray because it helps you focus on the life of Jesus and Mary and think about how much God loves us. As you pray, you'll learn about important events in their lives and understand how much they sacrificed for us. The Rosary is also a prayer of peace, where you can find calm and clarity. It's like taking a break from all the busyness of life to spend time thinking about God and feeling His presence.

When you pray the Rosary, you're asking Mary to help guide you closer to Jesus. She's a great example of faith, love, and obedience, and praying the Rosary helps you learn from her. Plus, it's a prayer you can do anytime—whether you're at home, outside, or even when you're waiting for something.

Chapter 11

Special Masses and Fun Celebrations

Mass is already a special time where we come together to worship God, listen to His Word, and receive Jesus in the Eucharist. But sometimes, there are special kinds of Masses that make the experience even more memorable! These special Masses are for different occasions in our lives, like weddings, funerals, and Holy Days. We also have important milestones in our faith, like First Communion and Confirmation, that are celebrated in a special way during Mass. In this chapter, we're going to dive into what makes these Masses so unique and why they're such important moments in our lives.

Weddings, Funerals, and Holy Days: What's Special About These Masses?

Mass is a time when we gather to worship God, but sometimes the reason for gathering is extra special. Let's take a look at some of the occasions that make certain Masses stand out: weddings, funerals, and Holy Days. Each of these celebrations adds something unique to the Mass and helps us focus on different parts of life and faith.

Weddings: Celebrating Love and New Beginnings

Weddings are one of the most joyful celebrations in the Church! When two people decide to get married, they're making a promise to each other and to God that they will love and support each other for the rest of their lives. A wedding Mass is a beautiful ceremony where a couple gets married in the presence of God and the Church community.

During a wedding Mass, the couple doesn't just exchange rings and vows, they also ask for God's blessing on their marriage. The priest leads them in prayers, and the couple receives Holy Communion together, showing that their love is rooted in God's love. This is a special way of saying, "God, please bless us as we begin this new chapter of our lives."

The wedding Mass also reminds us of God's plan for love. The priest talks about how marriage is a sacrament—an important sign of God's love for us. Just like God loves us, the couple promises to love each other in a way that reflects that same love. Wedding Masses are full of joy, prayer, and celebration because they're not just about the couple—they're about how God is at the center of their love and their future together.

Funerals: Honoring Life and Saying Goodbye

While weddings are joyful celebrations, funerals are a time when we come together to remember and honor someone who has passed away. A funeral Mass is a time for the family and friends of the person who has died to pray together and ask God to welcome their loved one into Heaven. It's a time to celebrate the life of the person and reflect on how they touched the lives of others.

During the funeral Mass, we pray for the person who has passed and thank God for the gift of their life. We also ask God to comfort the grieving family and friends. The priest leads prayers for the deceased, and the family may share special readings or memories. The Eucharist is offered as a way to invite the person's spirit into God's love and care.

Funeral Masses remind us that death is a part of life, but it's not the end. As Christians, we believe that there is eternal life with God in Heaven, and the funeral Mass is a way of affirming that belief. Even though funerals can be sad, they also offer hope because they remind us that God is always with us, even in difficult times. The Mass helps us pray for the person who has died and offers peace to those left behind.

Holy Days: Celebrating Special Events in the Church's Calendar

Throughout the year, the Church celebrates special Holy Days that focus on important events in the life of Jesus and the saints. These Masses are special because they focus on the big moments of our faith that shape how we live. For example, Christmas and Easter are two of the most important Holy Days. On Christmas, we celebrate the birth of Jesus, and on Easter, we celebrate His resurrection.

Other Holy Days might include the Assumption of Mary, the Feast of the Immaculate Conception, and the Feast of All Saints. Each of these days has its own special Mass, and the readings, prayers, and songs will help us remember the importance of these events. Holy Days are a time to pause and focus on what God has done for us through Jesus and the saints.

These Masses are different from regular Sundays because they celebrate something special about our faith. Sometimes, people will have a Holy Day Mass on a weekday, and even though it's not a Sunday, it's still a chance to come together and celebrate God's goodness. Holy Days are special times when the whole Church gets to celebrate as one.

First Communion and Confirmation:
What Happens at These Important Days?

Now let's talk about two big moments in your life as a young Catholic: First Communion and Confirmation. These two milestones mark important steps in your faith journey, and they are celebrated with special Masses that are unforgettable!

First Communion: Receiving Jesus for the First Time

First Communion is one of the most exciting and special days in the life of any child who is preparing to receive Jesus in the Eucharist for the first time. The Eucharist is the Body and Blood of Jesus, and it's the most important gift God gives us. When you receive First Communion, you are welcoming Jesus into your heart in a new and powerful way.

Before your First Communion, you will likely attend religious education classes to learn about what the Eucharist is and why it's so special. You will learn that when you receive Communion, it's not just a piece of bread—it's Jesus Himself. The priest or Eucharistic minister will say, "The Body of Christ," and you will respond, "Amen," which means, "Yes, I believe."

On your First Communion day, you'll wear a special outfit—often a white dress or suit—to show that you are ready to receive Jesus with a pure heart. During the Mass, you'll walk up to the altar with your family and friends, and when you receive the Eucharist for the first time, you're not just eating bread—you're connecting with Jesus in a special way. It's like receiving a hug from God and saying, "Thank You, Jesus, for being with me."

First Communion is a day of great joy and celebration because it's not just about receiving Jesus—it's also about growing in your relationship with Him. After receiving Communion, you can feel closer to Jesus, and you can continue to grow in faith by attending Mass regularly and receiving Communion every week.

Confirmation: Strengthening Your Faith

Confirmation is another huge step in your faith journey. While First Communion is about receiving Jesus for the first time, Confirmation is about receiving the Holy Spirit in a special way to help you live out your faith. It's like getting a special gift from God that helps you live stronger and more fully for Him.

Confirmation is a sacrament where the bishop (or sometimes the priest) lays his hands on your head and anoints you with holy oil, called chrism, to mark you as a follower of Christ. The bishop says, "Be sealed with the gift of the Holy Spirit," and you respond, "Amen." This moment is a way of saying, "I'm ready to be a stronger follower of Jesus, and I accept the help of the Holy Spirit to guide me in life."

The Holy Spirit is like a helper who gives you the strength to live your faith every day. When you are confirmed, you are saying, "Yes, I want to be fully part of God's family, and I'm ready to share my faith with others." It's a big moment in your life when you say, "I choose to follow Jesus, and I want to live as a true Christian."

Each of these Masses—weddings, funerals, Holy Days, First Communion, and Confirmation—helps us celebrate different parts of life and faith. Weddings celebrate love and new beginnings, while funerals help us honor a life and remember God's promise of eternal life. Holy Days let us stop and reflect on the big moments of our faith, and First Communion and Confirmation are milestones that help you grow closer to God and become more involved in the Church.

What makes these Masses so special is that they connect us with each other and with God. Whether you're celebrating a wedding, remembering a loved one who has passed away, or receiving a sacrament, each of these Masses reminds us that we are all part of God's family. These celebrations help us grow in love, hope, and faith, and they bring us closer to God, just as He wants us to be.

So, whether you're at a wedding, celebrating your First Communion, or attending a Holy Day Mass, remember that each of these special Masses is a moment to celebrate God's love and to connect with the whole Church. Each Mass is a chance to thank God for the big and small moments in life and to ask for His help and blessings in everything we do.

Chapter 12

How to Get Ready for Mass

Mass is a time to connect with God, learn from His Word, and receive His love through the Eucharist. But before you can fully experience the power of Mass, it's important to get ready—not just physically, but also with your heart and mind. In this chapter, we'll talk about how you can prepare for Mass so that you're fully ready to hear God's message and experience His presence. We'll also discuss how to act during Mass, including posture, gestures, and what to wear, so you can show your respect and love for God while you're there.

Preparing Your Heart and Mind Before Mass

Mass isn't just about going through the motions—it's about connecting with God and entering into a sacred time of prayer. So, getting your heart and mind ready before Mass is super important. You might be excited to go or maybe a little distracted by everything else happening around you. Whatever the case, here are some ways to help prepare before you even step foot in the church.

1. Quiet Time for Reflection

Before you even arrive at church, take a few moments to quiet your mind. It's easy to get caught up in the busy parts of the day, like homework, sports, or screen time. But when you're getting ready to go to Mass, it's good to take a moment to slow down and focus. You can do this in your car, before you leave your house, or even in the church before Mass starts. Think about the reason why you're going: to spend time with God, to worship, and to receive Jesus in the Eucharist. If you're feeling anxious, worried, or excited about something, take a deep breath and ask God to help you focus on Him during Mass. You can also say a little prayer, like, "God, I'm here for You. Help me be present and open to what You want to teach me today."

2. Reflect on the Readings

If you want to get even more prepared, check out the readings for Mass before you go. You can find them online or in a Mass booklet at church. The readings tell us about God's message for the day, and it can be helpful to know what they're about before Mass starts. This way, when you hear them in church, you can listen with more attention. For example, if the

Gospel is about forgiving others, think about the people in your life you need to forgive or who might need forgiveness from you. Being ready like this will make the readings feel more meaningful when they're read at Mass.

3. Be Ready to Give Thanks

Mass is a time of thanksgiving. We're there to show God how thankful we are for all He's done in our lives. Whether you've had a tough week or an amazing one, Mass is a time to put everything into perspective and say, "Thank You, God." You might have worries or challenges, but when you enter Mass, try to remember all the blessings you've received. It could be your family, your health, the ability to learn new things, or the love of your friends. By taking time to thank God, you prepare your heart to be open to His love and teaching.

How to Act During Mass: Posture, Gestures, and What to Wear

Now that your heart and mind are ready, it's time to focus on how to act during Mass. Everything you do during Mass—whether you're standing, sitting, kneeling, or even just how you dress—helps you show your love and respect for God. Here are some tips on posture, gestures, and what to wear so that you can participate fully in the Mass.

1. Posture: Standing, Sitting, and Kneeling

Mass involves a lot of movement—standing, sitting, and kneeling—and each one has a special meaning. It's important to pay attention to these movements because they help you focus on God and show Him respect.

- Standing: You stand when it's time to listen to the Gospel or when the priest is offering prayers. Standing is a sign of respect and readiness. It's like when you stand up to listen to someone important speak or to show that you're paying attention. So when you stand at Mass, remember that you're standing to show God you're ready to listen to His Word and be part of the celebration.

- Sitting: You sit during the readings and the homily. Sitting helps you focus and listen. It's a more relaxed position, but it's also a time to reflect on what's being said. You're not just sitting for the sake of sitting—you're sitting because you want to absorb the words of God and think about how they apply to your life.

- Kneeling: Kneeling is an important gesture of reverence and prayer.

You kneel during the Eucharistic Prayer to show deep respect for Jesus' presence. Kneeling helps us remember how awesome and holy God is, and it's also a way to show humility. Kneeling says, "God, I recognize You are greater than I am, and I honor You for all You've done."

2. Gestures: Showing Respect and Reverence

Mass is not just about what we say, but also about what we do. Your gestures show God your love, respect, and willingness to be part of the celebration. Here are some important gestures to remember during Mass:

- The Sign of the Cross: Every time you make the Sign of the Cross, you're reminding yourself of the Holy Trinity—God the Father, the Son (Jesus), and the Holy Spirit. The Sign of the Cross is a powerful way to start or end a prayer. It's also a way to show that you belong to God, and you trust Him with your life.

- Bowing: You might notice people bowing their heads or bodies during certain moments of Mass, especially when the altar is mentioned or when the priest says something about God's name. Bowing is a sign of respect and honoring God's presence. It's a small gesture, but it's a big way of showing God that you're humble before Him.

- Gestures during Communion: When you go up for Communion, you might see others bowing or making the Sign of the Cross. These small gestures help us stay focused and reverent as we prepare to receive Jesus. Remember to say "Amen" when you receive the Body of Christ—this shows that you believe in what you're receiving and are thankful for the gift.

3. What to Wear: Dressing Respectfully for Mass

How you dress for Mass is important, too. While the clothes you wear don't change how God loves you, dressing in a respectful way helps you show reverence for the sacred time you're spending in church.

- Dress neatly: When you dress for Mass, try to wear something nice or clean. You don't need to wear fancy clothes, but it's good to wear something that helps you focus on God. If you're comfortable and put together, it can help you feel ready to worship.

- Dress appropriately: Sometimes, we can get distracted by clothes that are too casual or not respectful. It's important to wear clothes that allow you to participate fully in Mass without distraction. Think about it this way—if you were going to a special event or meeting someone you really respect, you'd want to dress nicely, right? The same goes for Mass—dress in a way that honors the sacredness of the time you're spending with God.

- Remember your attitude matters more than your clothes: While wearing something nice is good, remember that your heart is the most important part of getting ready for Mass. What's inside you—your love, respect, and desire to connect with God—is what really matters. So even if you're in your favorite comfy clothes, as long as you're ready to worship and be respectful, that's what counts!

- Getting ready for Mass isn't just about following rules or looking good—it's about showing respect and love for God. When you prepare your heart and mind before Mass, you're opening yourself up to God and saying, "I'm here to listen to You and grow closer to You." By paying attention to posture and gestures during Mass, you're showing that you're truly participating and honoring the sacred time.

- How you dress also shows that you're taking Mass seriously. It's not just a routine—it's a time to meet God, listen to His Word, and be fed spiritually. Whether you're standing, sitting, or kneeling, each movement is a way to show that you're ready to focus on God and give Him your full attention.

- Mass is a special time where you get to be part of God's family, and getting ready for it helps you make the most of that time. So next time you go to Mass, remember that everything you do, from preparing your heart to the way you act and dress, helps you connect with God and worship Him in the best way possible.

Chapter 13

What the Eucharist Really Means

When you go to Mass, you might hear a lot of talk about the Eucharist, especially when it's time for Communion. You've probably seen people walk up to the altar, and the priest says, "The Body of Christ," and they respond, "Amen," before receiving the bread. But what does Eucharist really mean, and why is it such an important part of Mass? In this chapter, we're going to explore what the Eucharist really is, what it means to have Jesus in our hearts, and how the stories of Jesus in the Bible help us understand the Eucharist even better. Plus, we'll look at how Jesus teaches us to live through the Eucharist. Let's dive in!

What is the Eucharist? Jesus in Our Hearts

The Eucharist is one of the most important gifts Jesus gave us. It's not just regular bread or wine. It's Jesus Himself! When we receive the Eucharist during Mass, we are receiving Jesus in a very real way. It's like inviting Him into our hearts, minds, and lives, all at once. Jesus, through the priest, offers Himself to us in the form of bread and wine. And even though it might look like bread, it's really Jesus' Body and the wine is really His Blood.

But how can this be? How can bread and wine turn into Jesus? This is a mystery, and mysteries are things that are hard to explain, but we believe because Jesus told us it's true. At the Last Supper, when Jesus shared His final meal with His friends, He took bread and said, "This is My body," and He took wine and said, "This is My blood." He didn't mean it in a figurative way; He was giving His actual self to them.

So when we go up to receive Communion at Mass, we're not just eating a snack, we're receiving Jesus. The Eucharist is a way to be close to Jesus. It's like when you spend time with a good friend. You talk to them, listen to them, and enjoy each other's company. When you receive the Eucharist, you're getting closer to Jesus and experiencing His love in a special way. It's a reminder that Jesus is always with us, not just in our thoughts, but in our hearts.

Stories of Jesus and the Eucharist: Biblical Foundations

To really understand what the Eucharist means, let's look at some stories from the Bible where Jesus explains what it's all about. One of the most important stories is from the Last Supper, when Jesus shared a meal with His friends before He died on the cross. This is the moment when Jesus gave the Eucharist to His disciples.

In the Gospel of Matthew, we read about the Last Supper, where Jesus takes the bread, breaks it, and shares it with His disciples. He says, "Take and eat; this is My body." Then He takes the cup of wine, gives thanks, and shares it with them, saying, "This is My blood of the covenant, which is poured out for many for the forgiveness of sins" (Matthew 26:26-28). This moment is incredibly special because it's the first time Jesus gives His Body and Blood in the form of bread and wine.

But that wasn't the only time Jesus talked about the Eucharist. In the Gospel of John, there's a story called the Bread of Life Discourse. Jesus says to the people, "I am the bread of life; whoever comes to Me will never go hungry, and whoever believes in Me will never be thirsty" (John 6:35). Later, He says something that really gets people thinking: "Unless you eat the flesh of the Son of Man and drink His blood, you have no life in you" (John 6:53). This might sound strange, but what Jesus is telling us is that His body and blood are essential for our spiritual life. It's through the Eucharist that we receive Jesus, the Bread of Life, and that gives us the strength to live out our faith.

The Eucharist is a gift that has been passed down from generation to generation, starting with Jesus and His disciples. Jesus didn't just say these words for them, He said them for all of us. Every time we receive Communion, we are sharing in the same meal that Jesus shared with His friends, and we're joining in the mystery of His love for us. It's a powerful reminder that Jesus is always with us, and that He wants to nourish us with His very self.

Learning from Jesus: How He Teaches Us to Live

The Eucharist isn't just about receiving Jesus; it's also about learning how to live like Him. Jesus gave us the Eucharist to help us stay close to Him and to show us how to live in a way that brings God's love to the world. When we receive the Eucharist, we're not just getting filled up with God's love for ourselves, we're also being sent out into the world to share that love with others.

Jesus teaches us to live with love, compassion, and kindness. Think about how He lived His life. He cared for the sick, helped the poor, and showed kindness to everyone, especially those who were left out or forgotten.

Jesus didn't just say, "Love one another." He showed us how to love with His actions. Every time you receive the Eucharist, you're reminded that Jesus loved you first, and now you're called to share that love with others.

For example, in the Last Supper story, Jesus also washes His disciples' feet. He shows them that being a leader in God's kingdom is not about being the boss or getting attention; it's about serving others with humility and love. When you receive the Eucharist, it's like Jesus is saying, "Take this love and go out into the world, just like I did. Serve others. Love others. Help others." The Eucharist strengthens us to do just that, to live like Jesus and spread His love wherever we go.

In the Gospel of John, when Jesus talks about being the Bread of Life, He says, "Whoever eats this bread will live forever" (John 6:58). This is a promise that goes beyond just physical bread. Jesus is saying that when we receive Him, He gives us eternal life, a life full of love, joy, and peace. This doesn't just mean life after we die; it means living a full, meaningful life here and now. When you receive Jesus in the Eucharist, you're not just getting a spiritual snack. You're receiving the strength to live the life God wants for you.

The Eucharist and Our Actions

When you receive the Eucharist, you're receiving much more than just a piece of bread and wine. You're receiving Jesus Himself. This is a powerful and sacred moment, but it's also a reminder that receiving Jesus should change how we live. If you eat a healthy meal, it gives you energy, right? Well, the Eucharist gives us spiritual energy to live out the love of Jesus in the world.

After you receive Communion, think about how you can share the love and kindness you've received. Maybe it's by helping someone in need, saying something kind to a friend, or forgiving someone who has hurt you. The Eucharist calls you to live differently, not just for yourself, but for others. It teaches you to love like Jesus loves and to make the world a better place by spreading God's love.

The Eucharist is the heart of our faith because it connects us directly with Jesus. Every time we receive the Eucharist, we are reminded of God's incredible love for us. But it's not just about the moment when we receive the bread and wine. It's about how the Eucharist changes us and empowers us to live more like Jesus. The Eucharist helps us stay close to God, reminds us of the sacrifice Jesus made for us, and gives us the strength to spread His love everywhere we go.

So, when you're at Mass, remember that receiving the Eucharist isn't just a ritual, it's a gift from God. It's God giving you His love and strength to help you live a life of faith. It's an invitation to live with love, kindness, and forgiveness, just like Jesus did. And every time you receive the Eucharist, you're reminded that Jesus is always with you, in your heart, ready to guide you in everything you do.

Chapter 14

Living the Mass Every Day

Mass is a special time to come together, listen to God's Word, and receive Jesus in the Eucharist. But the truth is, Mass doesn't have to stay inside the church. Everything we hear, do, and experience at Mass is meant to be lived out every day. God doesn't just want us to show up at church once a week; He wants to be part of our lives all the time. So, how can we bring what we learn at Mass into our everyday lives? In this chapter, we'll talk about how you can think about what you hear at Mass, spend time with Jesus outside of church, and bring the love of Jesus into your daily routine.

Thinking About What We Hear at Mass

When you're at Mass, there are so many things going on. You hear the priest's homily, listen to the Bible readings, and sing songs of praise. But do you ever wonder how to make sense of it all and think about it after Mass? One of the most important things you can do is reflect on what you hear during Mass. Reflection means taking some time to think about what you've learned and how it can apply to your life.

After Mass, think about the Gospel reading, the story about Jesus. What did He do in the story? What can you learn from Him? For example, if the Gospel was about Jesus showing love to others, you can ask yourself, "How can I show love to others today?" Or, if the reading was about forgiveness, think about someone you may need to forgive or ask for forgiveness from. This is how you make what you heard at Mass really stick with you. It's not just about listening to a story or prayer, but about taking those lessons and living them out in your daily life.

You can also reflect on the prayers said during Mass. When you say the Our Father or the Hail Mary, think about the words and their meaning. The Our Father asks God to give us what we need, forgive us, and keep us safe. After Mass, you can reflect on what you need to ask God for and what you need to forgive or be forgiven for. The Hail Mary helps you remember that Mary is there to pray for you. Think about how you can ask her for help when you need it.

Mass is a time to receive God's love, but it's also a time to think about how to carry that love into the rest of your life. Reflection is a powerful way to make the lessons from Mass live on in your heart.

Spending Time with Jesus: Eucharistic Adoration

The Eucharist is such a special part of Mass. It's when we receive the Body and Blood of Jesus, which is the most amazing gift we could ever receive. But did you know that there's also a way to spend time with Jesus even after Mass is over? It's called Eucharistic Adoration, and it's a wonderful way to grow closer to Jesus.

Eucharistic Adoration is when the Eucharist, or the Blessed Sacrament (the consecrated Host), is placed in a special holder called a Monstrance, and people can come to spend time in prayer before it. The Blessed Sacrament is Jesus, the same Jesus you receive at Communion, and now you can spend time with Him.

When you go to Eucharistic Adoration, you can sit quietly and pray, talk to Jesus, or just be with Him. You don't have to say anything if you don't feel like it. You can just sit in silence and feel the love that Jesus has for you. It's like spending time with a friend, where you can talk if you want, but it's also okay just to be with them.

During Eucharistic Adoration, you're reminded that Jesus is always with you, even when you're not at Mass. He's there, waiting for you to come and spend time with Him. It's a quiet time of peace and love where you can get closer to Jesus, just like when you have a quiet moment to talk with a close friend.

If you've never been to Eucharistic Adoration, you might want to talk to your parents or your priest about going. It's a great way to get more out of what you experience at Mass and to keep Jesus close to your heart every day. Even if you can't go often, just knowing that Jesus is always there for you in the Blessed Sacrament can make a huge difference in your faith.

Bringing Jesus into Your Life Every Day

The best part about Mass is that it doesn't end when the final blessing is given. Jesus goes with you. The love and strength you receive from the Eucharist doesn't stay in church—it can be with you every single day. But how can you bring Jesus into your life all the time? Here are some ways:

1. Being Kind to Others

One of the most important ways to bring Jesus into your daily life is by showing love and kindness to the people around you. Jesus loved everyone, no matter who they were. He helped the poor, healed the sick, and showed kindness to people others might not have cared about. When you help others, whether it's your family, your friends, or even strangers, you are sharing the love that you receive from Jesus at Mass.

For example, if someone at school is feeling left out, you can be kind and invite them to join in. Or, if you see someone who is upset, you can offer them a listening ear. These small acts of kindness show that you're living out the love you've received from Jesus. Jesus wants you to love others the way He loves you, and that's the best way to share the Eucharist in your life.

2. Forgiving Others

Forgiveness is another way to bring Jesus into your life. In the Our Father, we ask God to forgive us just as we forgive others. That means that when someone hurts you or makes you upset, instead of staying angry, you can choose to forgive them, just like Jesus forgives you. It can be hard to forgive sometimes, but the Eucharist gives you the strength to do it. Every time you receive Communion, you're reminded of Jesus' forgiveness and love. By forgiving others, you're living out His love and showing how much you've learned from Him.

3. Praying Every Day

Mass is a great time to pray, but you can pray every day, too! You don't have to wait until next Sunday to talk to God. You can pray in the morning, before bed, or anytime you feel the need. Even if it's just a quick prayer like, "Jesus, thank You for today. Please help me be kind," you're making time for God in your life. Prayer keeps you connected to God and helps you remember that He's with you all the time, not just when you're at Mass.

4. Helping Others at Home

Jesus taught us to serve others. He washed His disciples' feet to show them that the greatest leaders are the ones who help others. You can do this at home by helping your parents, cleaning up without being asked, or helping a sibling with something. When you help others, you're living out the lesson of service that Jesus taught us. Your actions reflect the love you've received from the Eucharist and spread it to others.

5. Being a Light in the World

Jesus said that we are the light of the world (Matthew 5:14). This means that you can shine with His love wherever you go. Whether it's in school, at home, or with your friends, you can be a good example of Jesus by being positive, kind, and helpful. Every time you share His love, you are bringing Jesus into your everyday life.

Why It's Important to Live the Mass Every Day

Living the Mass every day means more than just remembering the prayers or songs you heard in church—it means living out what you experienced. It's about taking the love you felt when you received Communion and sharing it with the world. The Eucharist isn't just a moment in church; it's a way of life. Every time you pray, help others, or forgive someone, you are showing the love of Jesus.

Jesus didn't just come to us once—He stays with us. He gave us the Eucharist so we could always be connected to Him. By living the lessons of Mass every day, you are carrying Jesus with you and being His hands and feet in the world. You're not just a follower of Jesus during Mass—you're a follower all the time.

So, when you leave Mass, remember that Jesus is in your heart and wants you to share His love with everyone around you. Whether it's through acts of kindness, prayer, or forgiveness, living the Mass every day helps you grow in your faith and bring Jesus into the world. The Eucharist gives you the strength to love others, follow Jesus, and be a light in the world.

Remember, Mass isn't just a one-time event—it's a way of life. And every time you receive Jesus, you can take that love with you, knowing He's always by your side, ready to help you live out His teachings in the world.

Bonus: Quick-Reference List

This section gathers all of the people's parts in the order in which they appear at Mass. It allows the faithful to follow the entire liturgy without confusion and to participate fully with their voices and gestures. Each response is short, but together they form the prayer of the whole Church.

Introductory Rites

Sign of the Cross

Priest: *In the name of the Father, and of the Son, and of the Holy Spirit.*

People: *Amen.*

Greeting

Priest: *The Lord be with you.*

People: *And with your spirit.*

Penitential Act

People (Confiteor): *I confess to almighty God...*

Priest: *Lord, have mercy.*

People: *Lord, have mercy.*

Priest: *Christ, have mercy.*

People: *Christ, have mercy.*

Priest: *Lord, have mercy.*

People: *Lord, have mercy.*

Gloria (when prescribed)

People: *Glory to God in the highest...* (recited or sung together).

Collect

Priest: *Let us pray.*

People: *Amen.*

Liturgy of the Word

First and Second Readings

Reader: *The Word of the Lord.*

People: *Thanks be to God.*

Responsorial Psalm

Cantor: verse of the psalm.

People: refrain response (e.g., *The Lord is my shepherd; there is nothing I shall want.*).

Gospel Acclamation

People: *Alleluia* (or a seasonal acclamation during Lent).

Gospel Reading

Deacon/Priest: *The Lord be with you.*

People: *And with your spirit.*

Deacon/Priest: *A reading from the holy Gospel according to N.*

People: *Glory to you, O Lord.*

At the end: *The Gospel of the Lord.*

People: *Praise to you, Lord Jesus Christ.*

Homily – no response.

Profession of Faith (on Sundays and solemnities)

People: *I believe in one God...* (Nicene Creed or Apostles' Creed).

Prayer of the Faithful

Reader: *We pray to the Lord.*

People: *Lord, hear our prayer.*

Liturgy of the Eucharist

Presentation of the Gifts

Priest: *Pray, brothers and sisters, that my sacrifice and yours may be acceptable to God, the almighty Father.*

People: *May the Lord accept the sacrifice at your hands for the praise and glory of his name, for our good and the good of all his holy Church.*

Preface Dialogue

Priest: *The Lord be with you.*

People: *And with your spirit.*

Priest: *Lift up your hearts.*

People: *We lift them up to the Lord.*

Priest: *Let us give thanks to the Lord our God.*

People: *It is right and just.*

Sanctus

People: *Holy, Holy, Holy Lord God of hosts…*

Memorial Acclamation (after consecration)

Priest: *The mystery of faith.*

People (choose one):

> *We proclaim your Death, O Lord, and profess your Resurrection until you come again.*
>
> *When we eat this Bread and drink this Cup, we proclaim your Death, O Lord, until you come again.*
>
> *Save us, Savior of the world, for by your Cross and Resurrection you have set us free.*

Doxology and Great Amen

Priest: *Through him, and with him, and in him…*

People: *Amen.*

Communion Rite

Lord's Prayer

People: *Our Father, who art in heaven…*

Embolism Response

Priest: *Deliver us, Lord, we pray…*

People: *For the kingdom, the power and the glory are yours now and forever.*

Sign of Peace

Priest: *The peace of the Lord be with you always.*

People: *And with your spirit.*

Agnus Dei

People: *Lamb of God, you take away the sins of the world, have mercy on us… grant us peace.*

Communion

Minister: *The Body of Christ.*

People: *Amen.*

Minister: *The Blood of Christ.*

People: *Amen.*

Concluding Rites

Blessing

Priest: *The Lord be with you.*

People: *And with your spirit.*

Priest: *May almighty God bless you, the Father, and the Son, and the Holy Spirit.*

People: *Amen.*

Dismissal

Deacon/Priest: *Go forth, the Mass is ended.* (or another formula).

People: *Thanks be to God.*